Totus Tuus, Maria

Twelve days of preparation for consecration to Our Lady
Deepening the spiritual life in accordance with the
teaching of St Louis-Marie Grignion de Montfort

To the Immaculate Heart of Mary,
which has never ceased to beat
out of love for God and for men!

Totus Tuus, Maria

Personal Consecration to Our Lady
Following the Spiritual Teaching of
St Louis-Marie Grignion de Montfort

Florian Kolfhaus

GRACEWING

First published in Italian
under the title *Totus tuus, Maria. Dodici giorni di preparazione per la
consacrazione alla Madonna - Approfondimento della vita spirituale secondo i testi di
S. Luigi Maria Grignion da Montfort*
© Edizioni Cantagalli S.r.l., Siena—Italy, October 2011

Translated by Jan Bentz

First published in England in 2014
by
Gracewing
2 Southern Avenue
Leominster
Herefordshire HR6 0QF
United Kingdom
www.gracewing.co.uk

© 2014 Florian Kolfhaus

ISBN 978 085244 838 0

Typeset by Gracewing

Cover design by Bernardita Peña Hurtado

CONTENTS

PROLOGUE

"There is only one tragedy," said the French poet Léon Bloy, "and that is to not be a saint." Becoming a saint is indeed our life's goal; we are created for this. God has called the universe into being so that man might exist. He has breathed His life into Adam and Eve, making them the progenitors of His family. In order to fulfill His plan, He sent His own son, born of a woman (cf. Gal 4:4). He was crucified to free us from our sins, and He rose again that we might also live. Yes, the Father sent us His Son, who continues to be present in the Church throughout time, so as to give Him brothers and sisters. All that is, the whole cosmos, and all that God has done and continues to do, exists in order to make saints. Yes, only in them, the children of the heavenly Father, does the universe find meaning for its existence. As St. Paul states, "For the creation waits with eager longing for the revealing of the sons of God" (Rom 8:19).[1]

The world needs saints. Without them, without these men and women for whom it was made, it loses its most fundamental sense. Holiness, the life of God's children in communion with Him, is the goal of our entire existence; it is the goal of the whole cosmos. Indeed, there is no greater sorrow than to not become a saint. The success of all Nobel Prize winners and politicians, the glamour of Hollywood celebrities, and the victories of Olympic athletes wane in the light of even a single saint, as unknown and hidden as he might

---

1. English Standard Version.

be. That is why our world needs one thing above all else: holy men, women, and children who give God first place in their lives, and who give order and meaning not only to their own lives but to the whole of creation as well.

It is the tragedy of our time that the saints are often caricatured as bigots and pious actors, as people who do not know life and thus cannot enjoy it. The saint seems to be the moralizing ascetic, unworldly pariah, or naive dreamer. How wrong this is! St. Teresa Benedicta of the Cross (Edith Stein) wrote to her sister, "By the way, it is my conviction that it is not necessary for a saint to renounce all wishes and hopes of the world. Quite the opposite: man is in this world to live, and he is supposed to accept all the beautiful things that are given to him with gratitude." If holiness is the goal of our being, then the saints are indeed the ones who know this world and can rejoice in it because they have found the meaning for their existence and are aware of it. They are the ones who are truly happy in this world and in the next. The Latin word "beatus", meaning happy or blessed, indicates this: sanctity is a synonym of true and lasting happiness for which God has created us. In order not to lose sight of this goal, the world needs saints, men and women who have both of their feet on the ground but who have their gaze directed to heaven.

In essence, all men long for sanctity, for communion with God for whom they were created. A deep longing burns in all of us to understand the deepest roots of our being and to encounter the One who is Love. To love and to be loved—that is, in full offering, which is in God and possible for Him—is the deepest human longing; it is the fulfillment of that which we hope for as happiness and beatitude. The human heart is too large to be filled with anything less than God.

But what is a saint? There are many unfortunate misunderstandings that distort the image of true sanctity. Holiness is not a question of moral over-achievement or, even less, philistine philanthropy. To be holy, is—even before we start with our laborious task—a gift from God. "In baptism the Lord, as it were, sets our life alight with what the Catechism calls sanctifying grace. Those who watch over this light, who live by grace, are holy".[2] This task of our lives consists in saving that grace and increasing it. Yes, Baptism makes us Christian and demands of us that we live like Christ, that is, that we be saints.

St. Louis-Marie Grignion de Montfort understood this truth and did all he could to remind us of this glorious and great calling to sanctity. His *True Devotion to Mary*, which quickly became known as the *Golden Book*, is nothing other than a manual for becoming a saint. Louis-Marie is convinced that being a saint means living in the grace of Baptism, following Christ as a Christian. Who would be better suited to guide this journey than Mary, who—as a good mother—knows how she can help her children to live day by day as sons and daughters of Christ, and how to become ever more like her Son?

In this sense St. Louis-Marie Grignion de Montfort writes that saints are formed in Mary. In her, the greatest miracle happened: God became man. In her, as in a living tabernacle, Christ can be found. Everyone who trustfully consecrates himself to her will be formed in the image of the God-Man. She is, St. Louis-Marie writes, the easiest, quickest, most secure, and most perfect way to become a saint. Consecration to the Mother of God as a conscious renewal of one's baptismal vows was always highly recommended by the Church. St. Maximilian Kolbe declares, "Undoubtedly, all saints must be formed by the hands of the Virgin Mary. Why? Because all graces flow through the hands of this Most Holy Mother." The Curé of Ars is firmly convinced that all the saints, without exception, "have a great veneration for the Virgin, since

---

2. Pope Benedict XVI, *Address at the Vigil with young people*, Freiburg im Breisgau, September 24, 2011.

no grace comes down from heaven, except through her very
hands."

The Statue of Our Lady of Quito (Ecuador) depicts the
Mother of God as if dancing on the devil in the form of a
snake, while crushing its head, as foretold in the first book of
the Bible (cf. Gen 3:15). It is indeed extraordinary to show
Our Lady dancing. What does this image want to tell us? She
who is "full of grace" defeats evil effortlessly and joyfully.
It is God's grace in Mary's life, as in ours, which works great
things, if we only declare our *fiat* with the Virgin of Nazareth.
It is all about following Jesus by the hand of His Mother,
Mary. Even if we are not spared the Cross, it is not a life of
sadness and despair that awaits us, but a life of true joy and
hope. Consecrating oneself to Mary means, with reference to
the image of Quito, being led by this dance, which begins in
this world, but already follows the melody of heavenly music.
This is the core message of the "Golden Book": whoever
consecrates himself to Mary, as carefree as in dancing, will
make quicker and easier progress in the spiritual life and in the
struggle against one's faults, as with any other form of piety.
Consecration to Mary is, as it were, the prelude to a dance in
a truly Christian life, in which three steps are repeated over
and over again, and which the Mother teaches her children:
to know Jesus, to love Jesus, and to serve Jesus. Veneration
of Mary is not by any means secondary and, as some think,
not even really necessary. No! "Being Catholic means being
Marian".[3]

Often voices are heard which criticize consecration to
Mary as an exaggeration or see in it nothing other than senti-
mental piety. "De Maria numquam satis," the Church replies.
There can never be enough said about Mary; she can never be
honored enough. To God belongs our worship. Mary is and

---

3. Pope Benedict XVI, *Address to members of the Men's Marian Sodality of
   Regensburg*, May 28, 2011.

always remains a creature, but she is the masterpiece of the Divine Artist, who mirrors His perfection as nothing and no one in the entire universe. Mary is that which no other creature can say about itself: Mother of God. She is the only one who can call God "my child"! Consecrating oneself to Mary means nothing other than entering this dynamic of love and following the logic of the Incarnation. The saints have never feared to exaggerate veneration of Mary. Those who have consecrated themselves to the Mother of God call themselves—as if competing with one another—children of Mary, her servants, her slaves, her own property. Saint John Eudes says, "If I were to know someone who loves Mary more than I do, then I would hasten to that person—even hundred miles I would hasten—to learn how the Mother of God can be loved even more." Impressed by the Virgin Mary's beauty, Padre Pio, too, did not hesitate to declare, "Ah, my beautiful mommy, my dear mommy,... Jesus was right... Yes, you are beautiful... without the faith, men would call you a goddess... your eyes are more radiant than the sun... you are beautiful, mommy, it is my honor to love you." Consecration to Mary is not "Catholic kitsch" or a questionable form of piety, but the imitation of Christ through the hands of His mother, who safely guides anyone who entrusts himself to her. Therefore, the strong Catholic conviction is, "Servus Mariae numquam peribit," that is, "a servant of Mary will never perish."

St. Louis-Marie leads whomever wishes to consecrate himself to the Mother of God, and through her to her Divine Son, over thirty-three days toward the consecration. During this time, the faithful must decide to turn away from sin and strive to learn to love Jesus and Mary more. The fruit of this endeavor is supposed to be the conscious renewal of one's Baptismal vows, a complete giving of self to Jesus through Mary. The present work hopes to trace the steps of St. Louis-Marie Grignion and help the reader prepare himself for the consecration to Mary. In a conscious effort, the thirty-three days of this consecration have been reduced to twelve: three should serve as an in-depth examination of conscience and a renewal of life, and nine should serve as a novena to directly prepare for the consecration and to present the most important stages of Mary's life to the faithful.

At the end of the first three days a thorough confession is recommended, in which the penitent tries to look deeper into his life than in a typical confession. Hence, it is suggested to answer the questions of the examinations of conscience in written form and to prepare an in-depth confession with these written notes, perhaps even of one's entire past life. At the same time, one's gaze must be directed toward the future along with the question of fighting one's central flaw more effectively. The firm will to repent and concrete resolutions for the spiritual life are fruit of the first three days.

Each day of the Novena as a preparation for the consecration consists of two parts: one concerning prayer and one concerning reading. The part concerning prayer should serve as an opportunity to become closer to the Virgin Mother by meditating on her life and by entrusting oneself to her in prayer. To this end, the most common Marian prayers have been chosen in order for the faithful to acquire an array of prayers during this time. The principal part concerning prayer is one decade of the Rosary that should be prayed slowly and while meditating upon the images, which means meditating upon each mystery with one reason and heart. Obviously, it can be useful to pray the whole Rosary every day, but beginners in the spiritual life especially should avoid pushing themselves too hard. Someone who has never done sports cannot run a marathon. However, one who trains regularly and proceeds with reasonable steps can perform excellently without risking bruises or sprains. The same is true of the spiritual life, in which it is not prominently our own doing and working, but the effective grace of God.

Appended to the prayers and meditations for each day of the Novena is a reading with an excerpt taken from the *Golden Book* by St. Louis-Marie Grignion de Montfort. These readings contain a short introduction of the principal idea of the given meditation before the supplied text. At the end of the paragraph, the reader can find a biographical note of a saint and a prayer. The reading of these spiritual texts does not necessarily have to follow each meditation. It might be recommended to postpone this until another part of the day with time and inspiration. It is very reasonable to pause between the reading of these texts in order to consider and understand the thoughts of the different saints, and to make them one's own in prayer. It is also recommended to take notes of one's reflections and comments in a "spiritual diary."

This book has no other goal in mind than consecration to Our Lady according to St. Marie-Louis Grignion de Montfort: namely the quickest and most secure way to sanctity. It also assists the deepening of one's spiritual life. The countless hidden treasures that are contained in the Biblical texts and the writings of the saints must be uncovered and appropriated for oneself. One who has already been consecrated to Mary can fruitfully use this novena to prepare for the annual renewal of the consecration and to intensify his spiritual life.

It remains my sincere hope, that through this preparation for the consecration, many faithful might give themselves generously to the Mother of God, so that she in turn might bestow many saints upon our time. This book supports the main principle with which St. Louis-Marie Grignion de Montfort began his book: "Through Mary Christ came into this world; through Mary He wants to reign in this world!"

PREPARATION

My Life with God

The invocation of the Holy Spirit is recited as the initial prayer for each day.

Invocation of the Holy Spirit

Holy Spirit, Lord of light,
From Your clear celestial height
Your pure beaming radiance give.
Come, You Father of the poor,
Come with treasures which endure,
Come, You Light of all that live.

You, of all consolers best,
You, the soul's delightsome Guest,
Dost refreshing peace bestow.
You in toil art comfort sweet,
Pleasant coolness in the heat,
Solace in the midst of woe.

Light immortal, Light divine,
Visit You these hearts of Your,
And our inmost being fill.
If You take Your grace away,
Nothing pure in man will stay;
All his good is turned to ill.

Heal our wounds; our strength renew;
On our dryness pour Your dew;
Wash the stains of guilt away.
Bend the stubborn heart and will;
Melt the frozen, warm the chill;
Guide the steps that go astray.

You, on those who evermore
You confess and You adore,
In Your sevenfold gifts descend:
Give them comfort when they die,
Give them life with Your on high;
Give them joys that never end.
Amen.

Scripture Reading

Matthew 22: 2-14

The kingdom of heaven may be compared to a king who gave a wedding feast for his son, and sent his servants to call those who were invited to the wedding feast, but they would not come. Again he sent other servants, saying, 'Tell those who are invited, "See, I have prepared my dinner, my oxen and my fat calves have been slaughtered, and everything is ready. Come to the wedding feast."' But they paid no attention and went off, one to his farm, another to his business, while the rest seized his servants, treated them shamefully, and killed them.

The king was angry, and he sent his troops and destroyed those murderers and burned their city. Then he said to his servants, 'The wedding feast is ready, but those invited were not worthy. Go therefore to the main roads and invite to the wedding feast as many as you find.' And those servants went out into the roads and gathered all whom they found, both bad and good. So the wedding hall was filled with guests. "But when the king came in to look at the guests, he saw there a man who had no wedding garment. And he said to him, 'Friend, how did you get in here without a wedding garment?' And he was speechless. Then the king said to the attendants, 'Bind him hand and foot and cast him into the outer darkness. In that place there will be weeping and gnashing of teeth.' For many are called, but few are chosen."

Reflection

Out of pure love God has created each individual human being. Nothing would lack His divine beatitude if we did not exist. Nevertheless, God "yearns" for our love and waits, since He has given us the marvelous gift of freedom, for our personal response. He created us without our own doing, but He wants to redeem us with our collaboration. This collaboration is characterized by our acceptance of the invitation to the heavenly wedding feast and the will not to prefer anything else before it. School, work, family, and leisure time are all good and important; more important is God's calling. Our answer consists of regular prayer, seeking His will and making an effort to do the good, to receive the Sacraments with faith and zeal; in a word, to love Him as He has commanded us: "You shall love the Lord your God with all your heart and with all your soul and with all your might" (Dt 6:5)!

How sad it is that many people do not recognize that God prefers nothing to our happiness. God wants to have all people with Him in all eternity, but many do not answer Him. Indeed, they refute Him like stubborn children who do not want to believe that their father wants the best for them. God calls both the good and the bad into His kingdom; yes, with a special love He calls sinners and gives them the chance to repent. God does everything to see to it that we, at least at the last minute of our lives, can answer His love.

The answer is essential, however. Some give it by keeping their Baptismal gown stainless for their whole life and adorning it with good deeds; others, by repenting of their sins and accepting the new Baptismal gown in confession, which shines with the splendor of sanctifying grace. Without this gown there is no entry into heaven! Without this gown we must be ashamed of ourselves during the wedding feast before God and the other guests. As we would never dare enter a wedding feast on this earth like a beggar in rags, we would never enter the gate of heaven without festive attire. Let us try to keep our Baptismal gown spotless, or allow God to cleanse it again and again! Let us adorn it with many good deeds, that we may have ever-greater joy during the heavenly wedding feast!

(Brief silence and inner reflection)

Examination of conscience

My relation to God and His Church

- Have I tried to put God first in my life?
- Have I understood the sense and necessity of prayer, and have I made a determined time for it in my daily life?
- Do I try to listen to God's call and answer it?
- Have I made time for God? Do I pray with devotion, thankfulness, trust, and loving attention?
- Have I partaken in Mass every Sunday?
- Have I made an effort to receive communion fervently, or have I approached the supper of the Lord with indifference?
- Have I tried to avoid sin in my life and have I let myself be cleansed by God in confession?

- Have I thought about God, visited Him in Church, or have I completely forgotten Him?
- Have I willfully doubted God or the truths of faith?
- Have I tried to deepen my faith by reading good books from time to time, studying the Catechism, seeking spiritual guidance... or have I been indifferent to my knowledge of the faith?
- Am I proud of my faith and the Church, or have I authorized others to speak poorly of the faith and the Church?
- Have I fostered awe for God and holy things, or have I spoken with thoughtlessness of the Holy Name, even by cursing with it?
- Have I wished to be a friend of God and to orient my life in accordance with Him?
- Am I ready to let my daily life and my future be guided by God?
- What is my concrete resolution?

Penitential Psalm

Psalm 51

Have mercy on me, God, in your kindness.
  In your compassion blot out my offence.
O wash me more and more from my guilt
  and cleanse me from my sin.

My offenses truly I know them;
  my sin is always before me.
Against you, you alone, have I sinned;
  what is evil in your sight I have done.

That you may be justified when you give sentence
    and be without reproach when you judge,
O see, in guilt I was born,
    a sinner was I conceived.

Indeed you love truth in the heart;
    then in the secret of my heart teach me wisdom.
O purify me, then I shall be clean;
    O wash me, I shall be whiter than snow.

Make me hear rejoicing and gladness,
    that the bones you have crushed may revive.
From my sins turn away your face
    and blot out all my guilt.

A pure heart create for me, O God,
    put a steadfast spirit within me.
Do not cast me away from your presence,
    nor deprive me of your holy spirit.

Give me again the joy of your help;
    with a spirit of fervour sustain me,
that I may teach transgressors your ways
    and sinners may return to you.

O rescue me, God, my helper,
    and my tongue shall ring out your goodness.
O Lord, open my lips
    and my mouth shall declare your praise.

For in sacrifice you take no delight,
    burnt offering from me you would refuse,
my sacrifice, a contrite spirit.
    A humbled, contrite heart you will not spurn.

In your goodness, show favour to Zion:
   rebuild the walls of Jerusalem.
Then you will be pleased with lawful sacrifice,
   holocausts offered on your altar.

Glory be to the Father and to the Son and to the Holy Spirit,
   as it was in the beginning,
is now, and ever shall be,
   world without end. Amen.

Closing Prayer

Holy Spirit, You are the spirit of holiness, purity, and love! How can I stand before you after I have sinned? In Holy Baptism you have made my soul Your dwelling place through the infusion of sanctifying grace and have given me an immaculate baptismal gown, which I must keep for heaven. Time and time again, You have given me Your light, Your love, and Your caring help that I may keep it pure and spotless. Others who have collaborated with Your grace have become saints through You, heroes of the faith, and victors over their weaknesses. I stand as a sinner before You. How torn and dirty is my baptismal gown through sin! My God, I am ashamed to come before You like this, but I know that You are always ready to forgive me. I know that You love me. Forgive me my sins! Help me to resist temptations in the future. Under your guidance, and by the hand of Mary, I want to become a saint. Amen.

My relation to my neighbor

Invocation of the Holy Spirit

Holy Spirit, Lord of light,
From Your clear celestial height
Your pure beaming radiance give.
Come, You Father of the poor,
Come with treasures which endure,
Come, You Light of all that live.

You, of all consolers best,
You, the soul's delightsome Guest,
Dost refreshing peace bestow.
You in toil art comfort sweet,
Pleasant coolness in the heat,
Solace in the midst of woe.

Light immortal, Light divine,
Visit You these hearts of Yours,
And our inmost being fill.
If You take Your grace away,
Nothing pure in man will stay;
All his good is turned to ill.

Heal our wounds; our strength renew;
On our dryness pour Your dew;
Wash the stains of guilt away.
Bend the stubborn heart and will;
Melt the frozen, warm the chill;
Guide the steps that go astray.

You, on those who evermore
You confess and You adore,
In Your sevenfold gifts descend:
Give them comfort when they die,
Give them life with You on high;
Give them joys that never end.
Amen.

Scripture Reading

Matthew 25:31-41, 45 f

The Final Judgment

When the Son of Man comes in his glory, and all the angels
with him, then he will sit on his glorious throne. Before him
will be gathered all the nations, and he will separate people
one from another as a shepherd separates the sheep from
the goats. And he will place the sheep on his right, but the
goats on the left. Then the King will say to those on his
right, 'Come, you who are blessed by my Father, inherit the
kingdom prepared for you from the foundation of the world.
For I was hungry and you gave me food, I was thirsty and you
gave me drink, I was a stranger and you welcomed me, I was
naked and you clothed me, I was sick and you visited me, I
was in prison and you came to me.' Then the righteous will
answer him, saying, 'Lord, when did we see you hungry and
feed you, or thirsty and give you drink? And when did we see

you a stranger and welcome you, or naked and clothe you?
And when did we see you sick or in prison and visit you?'
And the King will answer them, 'Truly, I say to you, as you did
it to one of the least of these my brothers, you did it to me.'
Then he will answer them, saying, 'Truly, I say to you, as you
did not do it to one of the least of these, you did not do it to
me.' And these will go away into eternal punishment, but the
righteous into eternal life.

Thoughts for Contemplation

Everywhere we hear and read of social programs and
dedication to philanthropic acts, of tolerance, and justice.
People, too, who do not believe in God and or afterlife try to
make a better world, support minorities, or work to save the
environment. Does one have to profess Christ in order to be
a good person? Does it not suffice to not do evil?—No! What
Christ calls for in the Final Judgment requires more.

He does not simply ask that we become better people, but
that we truly love our neighbor. This is more than almsgiving!
It is about dedicating ourselves and giving ourselves in service
to others. Christian charity is more than benevolent action; it
is more than the commitment to a better world. True Christian charity is always the fruit of a true love of God. It surpasses the good works of those who do not believe, because
it requires the individual to step back, to renounce personal
advantages, to willingly forgive, to be patient and willing to
sacrifice. This attitude is fueled by the faith, by a deep friendship with Jesus, whom we may serve in the poorest of poor.
"To give until it hurts." This teaching of Mother Teresa is
only possible with the power of faith in a truly Christian magnanimity that enables us to give without counting, to give ourselves seeking nothing in return.

The passage of the Final Judgment of the world teaches us to perform concrete works of charity that the Church has summarized into the works of mercy—seven corporal: to feed the hungry, to give drink to the thirsty, clothe the naked, harbor the homeless, visit the sick, visit the imprisoned, and bury the dead; and seven spiritual: to instruct the ignorant, counsel the doubtful, admonish sinners, bear wrongs patiently, forgive offenses willingly, comfort the afflicted, and pray for the living and the dead. These twice seven works of Christian charity can be the measure of our examination of conscience, especially with regard to the often neglected questions of where we have failed to do good and failed to serve the Lord in the suffering brethren.

Of course, we do not always see Christ in the suffering before our eyes, especially not in those who are annoying and unlikeable to us. But when we overcome ourselves and try to do good, then we can look forward to the Final Judgment, when the Lord will reveal Himself to us: "Truly I tell you, whatever you did for one of the least of these brothers and sisters of mine, you did for me!" True charities will become the service of God! The saints, who are mentioned in the account of the world's judgment, practice love, so to speak, without thinking about it. They simply do it because that which fills their hearts flows over into their deeds. Wherever they see a need, they meet it. It is not only the commandment of Christ to which they feel obliged, as if they needed to remember at every moment what Christ wants from them. They do the good naturally, with dedication and spontaneity.

The just before Christ's throne of judgment do not seem to know that they served the Lord with their charity. Even more, their attitude seems to be the expression of a deep surprise and wonder about the fact that it was truly Jesus, whose sick body they cared for and whose loneliness they lessened through their visits. Almost with a certain distress they recognize how much the Lord of heaven has lowered Himself and suffered with the poor, sick, weak, and depressed. And the one who was condemned to death as an innocent, has indeed taken all the suffering of this world onto His cross. Before the judgment seat of Pilate, He bears all sin, sickness, fears, and the needs of men on His shoulders. As the coming Judge of the nations, He will call all the just who carried the cross with Him.

Let us draw strength for the daily dedication from knowing that He is the Lord to whom we do good. Let us remember that it is He whom we despise when we failed to do good to our neighbor. The Gospel passage about the final judgment says clearly that the sinners Christ condemns have altogether done nothing evil, or at least we do not hear about it, but their fault lies in that they have done nothing good. They have not proven their love to the Lord. Let us use the time to do good, because we will all be surprised in the last judgment that God does not forget even the slightest good deed, and that He will return every act of love one hundredfold, even if in the moment it seems like a small thing.

(Brief recollection)

Examination of Conscience:

My relation to my neighbor

- Do I try to do good unto others, or do I think primarily about my personal gain?

- Do I support the mission of charitable organizations?

- Do I pray for my parents, my relatives, my friends, and those who do me injustice?

- Do I support the needy around me with dedication?

- Am I courageous in speaking the truth?

- Am I able to remain silent if words would harm love?

- Do I try to see the good character traits of my fellow men, or do I simply look for their faults, perhaps to see myself in a better light?

- Am I hospitable? Do I approach those who are alone, alienated or difficult?

- Do I practice patience with others? Am I irascible, egotistical, or vain?

- Do I follow my superiors? Immediately and happily, or resentful and superficially?

- Do I take care of other people's goods?

- Am I a good friend? Do I wish good unto others, or do I think badly about them?

- Do I try to give a good example? What would I have to concretely change? Among those to whom I am close, who especially needs my help and my prayer?

Penitential Psalm

Psalm 130

Out of the depths I cry to you, O Lord,
    Lord, hear my voice!
O let your ears be attentive
    to the voice of my pleading.

If you, O Lord, should mark our guilt,
    Lord, who would survive?
But with you is found forgiveness:
    for this we revere you.

My soul is waiting for the Lord.
  I count on his word.
My soul is longing for the Lord
  more than watchman for daybreak.
Let the watchman count on daybreak
  and Israel on the Lord.

Because with the Lord there is mercy
  and fullness of redemption,
Israel indeed he will redeem
  from all its iniquity.

Glory be to the Father and to the Son and to the Holy Spirit,
  as it was in the beginning,
is now, and ever shall be,
  world without end. Amen.

Closing Prayer

O my Lord and my God, I have examined my conscience with Your grace. Allow me see the state of my soul in the light of faith, as You see it. Let me realize how I would stand before You, if today You would call me to judgment. Through Your illumination, let me realize how I have sinned in thoughts, words, and deeds, with my five senses, my memory, my intellect and will, the power of my body and my soul, and what good I have failed to do. Let me sincerely repent of it. Grant that I may love You above all things, because You are the highest and best Good, Who are loved above all things. Grant that I may love my neighbor for Your sake, and that I may seek to serve You in all my brothers and sisters who need me daily. Amen.

THIRD DAY

My Relation to Myself

Invocation of the Holy Spirit

Holy Spirit, Lord of light,
From Thy clear celestial height
Thy pure beaming radiance give.
Come, Thou Father of the poor,
Come with treasures which endure,
Come, Thou Light of all that live.

Thou, of all consolers best,
Thou, the soul's delightsome Guest,
Dost refreshing peace bestow.
Thou in toil art comfort sweet,
Pleasant coolness in the heat,
Solace in the midst of woe.

Light immortal, Light divine,
Visit Thou these hearts of Thine,
And our inmost being fill.
If Thou take Thy grace away,
Nothing pure in man will stay;
All his good is turned to ill.

Heal our wounds; our strength renew;
On our dryness pour Thy dew;
Wash the stains of guilt away.
Bend the stubborn heart and will;
Melt the frozen, warm the chill;
Guide the steps that go astray.

Thou, on those who evermore
Thee confess and Thee adore,
In Thy sevenfold gifts descend:
Give them comfort when they die,
Give them life with Thee on high;
Give them joys that never end.
Amen.

Scripture Reading

Matthew 25:14-30

The Parable of the Talents

For it will be like a man going on a journey, who called his
servants and entrusted to them his property. To one he gave
five talents, to another two, to another one, to each according
to his ability. Then he went away.

He who had received the five talents went at once and
traded with them, and he made five talents more. So also he
who had the two talents made two talents more. But he who
had received the one talent went and dug in the ground and
hid his master's money.

Now after a long time the master of those servants came
and settled accounts with them. And he who had received the
five talents came forward, bringing five talents more, saying,

'Master, you delivered to me five talents; here I have made five talents more.' His master said to him, 'Well done, good and faithful servant. You have been faithful over a little; I will set you over much. Enter into the joy of your master.' And he also who had the two talents came forward, saying, 'Master, you delivered to me two talents; here I have made two talents more.' His master said to him, 'Well done, good and faithful servant. You have been faithful over a little; I will set you over much. Enter into the joy of your master.'

He also who had received the one talent came forward, saying, 'Master, I knew you to be a hard man, reaping where you did not sow, and gathering where you scattered no seed, so I was afraid, and I went and hid your talent in the ground. Here you have what is yours.' But his master answered him, 'You wicked and slothful servant! You knew that I reap where I have not sown and gather where I scattered no seed? Then you ought to have invested my money with the bankers, and at my coming I should have received what was my own with interest. So take the talent from him and give it to him who has the ten talents. For to everyone who has will more be given, and he will have an abundance. But from the one who has not, even what he has will be taken away. And cast the worthless servant into the outer darkness. In that place there will be weeping and gnashing of teeth.

Reflection

God has given each one of us an array of talents and gifts. Some live in external wealth or have connections to move further ahead in life. Above all, God has given us the gift of sanctifying grace in Baptism. It is grace that makes us similar to Him and that will enable us to contemplate Him in heaven. But this sanctifying grace is not a possession that we should bury. In fact, God wants us to increase it by good deeds, frequent reception of the Sacraments, and patient acceptance of suffering and zealous work for His kingdom. The larger this treasure of sanctifying grace is within us, the greater also the glory of heaven will be for us: all men are totally happy beyond words in Heaven, since God wants to fill their soul-vessels with glory; but the larger we have made these vessels during our lifetime, the more they will be able to receive in the coming world. The more we love, the happier we will be! As servants of God we have to work with and increase all natural and supernatural gifts from God. Concretely, that means that God will ask us, if He has given us the talent of a musician, why we have not learned an instrument. We will have to justify why He gave us excessive wealth and we have not even used the interest of our riches to build His kingdom. We will have to give an account of whether we preferred a cozy, comfortable, well-behaved and bourgeois life—not much worse than many others—or whether we have put everything on the line for Him.

To avoid any misunderstanding, God does not call every person to enter a monastery and give away all of his belongings to the poor in order to take best advantage of his talents. Rather, God wants that each and every person, as a father of a family or a single teacher, as a gardener or professor, follow Christ in his occupation with all his strength and all of his talents; moreover, that everyone try hard to foster sanctifying grace through prayer, reception of the Sacraments and good works, and by doing so, to accumulate a treasure in Heaven, which no thief can steal (Cf. Math 6:20).

In the parable of the talents we can recognize once more that God demands more than just avoiding evil. The king even reproaches the servant for not having brought his talent to the bank where it would have created interest. If we apply this image to sanctifying grace, we can compare confession with the bank: every time Christ grants us forgiveness of our sins through the hands of a priest, He increases sanctifying grace in us. God rejoices that we return to Him and let His salvation take effect in us, that He may renew us in an even greater way than we were before the first fall. Jesus is the "Divine banker" who loves to divide His riches among those who truly love Him.

The Sacred Hearts of Jesus and Mary can be compared to a bank through which we receive abundant interest for our little balance. If we entrust to the Mother of God our treasure of sanctifying grace, which we carry in a fragile vessel (Cf. 2 Cor 4:7), our natural and supernatural goods will bear abundant fruit. Our Mother will not allow us to stand before our King at the end of our lives with empty hands and be afraid that He will discard us as happened to the lazy servant. Rather, on behalf of Mary, who will step before the throne as our advocate, Christ will call to us: "I have heard my mother speak of you. Come and partake in the happiness of your Lord!"
(Brief Recollection)

My relation to myself

- Do I strive to multiply my God-given talents, or do I bear them carelessly?

- Have I set high ideals and goals for myself (what are they?), or do I only think of myself, my pleasure, and my well-being?

- Do I ask God's will for my life, and do I seek to fulfill it?

- Am I too attached to sports, games, friends, entertainment, property, and money, or am I internally free for God and His plan for me?

- Am I miserly or wasteful?

- Am I irresponsible and "like a feather in the wind"?

- Do I strive to fight laziness, untidiness, and boredom in my life? Do I strive to do good?

- Am I willing to make sacrifices and renunciations? Do I fulfill my duties at home, at school, and at my job?

- Am I ready to conquer my senses and to fight curiosity, eating sweets, gluttony, gossip, and vanity?

- Am I responsible in my use of radio, television, and the Internet?

- Do I care for my body and strive for health? Do I avoid overexertion and idleness?

- Do I strive for purity and chastity? Do I keep my inner freedom in saying "no" to all that can enslave me?

- Do I keep distance from improper friends, films, magazines, and dubious entertainment?

- Am I truthful to myself and to others? Do I see myself in the right light, that is, am I humble, or do I overestimate myself?

- Do I care about external cleanliness and order?

- Do I trust in God's grace and that it can work things in me that I myself cannot attain, so that I can be trustful, calm, and hopeful even in situations of difficulty?

- Do I strive to strengthen my will through abstinence and effort? Do I let myself go, or do I have control of my passions and desires?

- What is my root sin? What can I concretely do to fight it? What sacrifice do I want to practice in order to concretely strengthen my will?

Penitential Psalm

Psalm 32

Happy the man whose offense is forgiven,
whose sin is remitted.
O happy the man to whom the Lord
imputes no guilt,
in whose spirit is no guile.

I kept it secret and my frame was wasted.
I groaned all day long,
for night and day your hand was heavy upon me.
Indeed my strength was dried up
as by the summer's heat.

But now I have acknowledged my sins;
my guilt I did not hide.
I said: "I will confess
my offense to the Lord."
And you, Lord, have forgiven
the guilt of my sin.

So let every good man pray to you
in the time of need.
The floods of water may reach high
but him they shall not reach.

You are my hiding place, O Lord;
you save me from distress.

Glory be to the Father and to the Son and to the Holy Spirit,
as it was in the beginning,
is now, and ever shall be,
world without end. Amen.

Closing Prayer

Beneficent God and Father, You are my Lord and my Creator. Out of pure love You have called me into being and preserved me in life. You desire that I partake of your eternal beatitude. Out of love You have given me the grace of the holy faith and You have granted me countless gifts, with which I am supposed to work for Your greater glory and which I must multiply. How faithful and thankful I should have been for that! But I have transgressed Your commandments; I have sinned and abandoned You. I have proven to be a poor servant and have oftentimes done evil. Even more often have I failed to do the good and what is best. Please forgive me! I despise my sins with my whole heart and I regret having offended You. Through the bitter suffering and death of Your son, Jesus Christ, and the co-suffering of His Holy Mother, Mary, please forgive me. Amen.

At the end of the three day preparatory period it is highly recommended to make a good confession in which not only are one's sins included, but also imperfections and false attitudes. If there is no priest available, the confession may be postponed. A strong effort should be made to receive the Sacrament of Confession before the end of the Novena and the following consecration to Mary.

NOVENA

Mary—The Immaculate Conception

After we have repented of our sins and confessed well, we can look ahead with a joyful heart; our guilt is annihilated, our sins forgiven, and they will carry no weight in the eyes of God.

That is why it is ever more important to begin our "new" life with magnanimity, without any compromises or half measures. The Novena before the Consecration to Mary should serve this purpose. Therefore, it is highly recommended to not only pray the given prayers during the following days, but to also look for a small sacrifice each day that we can offer to Mary. Every free sacrifice strengthens our will to the good. If we prepare the Consecration to the Mother of God with such zeal, then we can be assured that we will receive abundant graces from her; she has never been surpassed in her generosity and love.

Invocation of the Holy Spirit

Breathe in me, O Holy Spirit,
that my thoughts may all be holy.
Act in me, O Holy Spirit,
that my work, too, may be holy.
Draw my heart, O Holy Spirit,
that I love but what is holy.
Strengthen me, O Holy Spirit,
to defend all that is holy.

Guard me, then, O Holy Spirit,
that I may always be holy. Amen.

(St. Augustine)

Scripture Reading

Original sin

Genesis 3:9-15

"But the Lord God called to the man and said to him,
"Where are you?" And he said, "I heard the sound of you in
the garden, and I was afraid, because I was naked, and I hid
myself." He said, "Who told you that you were naked? Have
you eaten of the tree of which I commanded you not to eat?"
The man said, "The woman whom you gave to be with me,
she gave me fruit of the tree, and I ate." Then the Lord God
said to the woman, "What is this that you have done?" The
woman said, "The serpent deceived me, and I ate." The Lord
God said to the serpent, "Because you have done this, cursed
are you above all livestock and above all beasts of the field;
on your belly you shall go, and dust you shall eat all the days
of your life. I will put enmity between you and the woman,
and between your offspring and her offspring; she shall bruise
your head, and you shall bruise his heel."[4]

Reflection

Mary is mentioned in the first book of the Bible. God reveals
to Adam and Eve, who have lost paradise by their sin, that
they will be redeemed by Jesus Christ, who will come down

---

4. In the Vulgate version of the Holy Scriptures, which the Church has
   used for centuries in her liturgy, it is Mary who bruises the serpent's
   heel: "Ipsa conteret caput tuum." (Gen 3:15)

to earth. It is Mary who will bear the Savior; it is she through whom salvation will come to man. Her son is the enemy of the demonic serpent; she is the chosen woman who will crush the serpent's head!

Right after the victory that the devil claimed in Paradise, God prophesies his annihilation. He chooses a weak, but humble and pure girl, who will receive His Son to defeat the serpent—what a humiliation for the devil! Since Mary is at enmity with the devil, she is perfectly free from all sin; free of original sin, which has brought death and suffering in the world (cf. Rom 5:12). She is full of Grace; there is no room for sin in her, and all evil is repelled by her.

The Fathers of the Church call Mary the new Eve, since unlike our progenitrix, she is humble and obedient. Justice that we have lost because of Eve, has, through Mary, been brought back to the side of the new Adam, Jesus Christ, in a perfect manner. Eve sinned under the tree in Paradise; therefore, Christ had to die on the Cross for our transgressions. Mary, as the new Eve, and new Mother of all men, stands at the foot of the Cross, the true tree of life, and is the Mediatrix of all graces and all the fruits of salvation.

When on Golgotha the devil hurt Christ's heel—this "small" wound represents the death of Christ, which only lasts "three days." Mary crushes by grace of her Divine Son, the hellish serpent. When Jesus calls His mother "woman" in the face of the apostle, he calls in mind the prophecy of our redemption found in the first book of the Bible.

Let us rejoice in the fact that Mary, as the sinless One, the Immaculate, is the enemy of the serpent and the beloved friend of God. Indeed, she is all beautiful; no stain is on her! Let us ask her that we may become like her and that, through her intercession, we may find strength to avoid sin and to do good.

Decade of the Rosary

The third Joyful Mystery: The Birth of Jesus of the Blessed Virgin Mary in the stable at Bethlehem

We rejoice that God willed to give us Jesus, the Savior, through Mary, as He promised.

Prayer to the Mother of God

(Under Your Protection—Sub tuum praesidium)

We fly to your protection, O holy Mother of God. Despise not our petitions in our necessities, but deliver us always from all dangers O glorious and blessed Virgin.

Closing Prayer

Almighty God, through the Immaculate Conception you have prepared a worthy dwelling place for Your son; now we beseech you: As you have kept her, in view of the death of Your Son, from all stain of sin, let also us, by her intercession, reach You in a pure way. Through our Lord Jesus Christ, Your Son, who lives and reigns with You in the unity of the Holy Spirit, one God, forever and ever. Amen.

Spiritual Reading

True devotion to Our Lady

In what does the veneration of Mary consist? What is our attitude towards her? St. Louis-Marie Grignion de Montfort calls five qualities in mind, which are signs of the true devotion to Mary: interiority, trustfulness, holiness, constancy, disinterestedness! In short: Just like young children trust their mother unconditionally and love her with all their being, just like that we should love and trust Mary. When we love Mary in this way, then we can rejoice with our heart, since it is a sign of the true devotee to Mary, that he is a joyful child of his heavenly Mother.

From the *Treatise on True Devotion*

After having explained and condemned false devotions to the Blessed Virgin we shall now briefly describe what true devotion is. It is interior, trustful, holy, constant, and disinterested.

First, true devotion to Our Lady is interior, that is, it comes from within the mind and the heart and follows from the esteem in which we hold her, the high regard we have for her greatness, and the love we bear for her.

Second, it is trustful, that is to say, it fills us with confidence in the Blessed Virgin, the confidence that a child has for its loving mother. It prompts us to go to her in every need of body and soul with great simplicity, trust, and affection. We implore our Mother's help always, everywhere, and for everything. We pray to her to be enlightened in our doubts, to be put back on the right path when we go astray, to be protected when we are tempted, to be strengthened when we are weakened, to be lifted up when we fall into sin, to be encouraged when we are losing heart, to be rid of our scruples, and to be consoled in the trials, crosses and disappointments of life. Finally, in all our afflictions of body and soul, we naturally turn to Mary for help, never fearful of importuning her or displeasing our Lord.

Third, true devotion to Our Lady is holy, that is, it leads us to avoid sin and to imitate the virtues of Mary. Her ten principal virtues are: deep humility, lively faith, blind obedience, unceasing prayer, constant self-denial, surpassing purity, ardent love, heroic patience, angelic kindness, and heavenly wisdom.

Fourth, true devotion to Our Lady is constant. It strengthens us in our desire to do good and prevents us from giving up our devotional practices too easily. It gives us the courage to oppose the fashions and maxims of the world, the vexations and unruly inclinations of the flesh and the temptations of the devil. Thus, a person truly devoted to Our Blessed Lady is not changeable, fretful, scrupulous, or timid. We do not say, however, that such a person never sins or that his sensible feelings of devotion never change. When he has fallen, he stretches out his hand to his Blessed Mother and rises again. If he loses all taste and feeling for devotion, he is not at all upset because a good and faithful servant of Mary is guided in his life by faith in Jesus and Mary and not by feelings.

Fifth, true devotion to Mary is disinterested. It inspires us to seek God alone in His Blessed Mother and not ourselves. The true subject of Mary does not serve his illustrious Queen for selfish gain. He does not serve her for temporal or eternal well-being, but simply and solely because she has the right to be served, and God alone in her. He loves her not so much because she is good to Him or because He expects something from her, but simply because she is lovable. That is why He loves and serves her just as faithfully in weariness and dryness of soul as in sweet and sensible fervor. He loves her as much on Calvary as at Cana.[5]

From the Lives of the Saints

St. Maximilian Kolbe

On January 7, 1894, Raymond Kolbe was born in the part of Poland that was occupied by the Russians. Together with his brothers Franz and Josef he received a rather austere education. Raymond was very lively and always ready for mischief. He worried his mother a lot. One day, she sighed:

---

5. *True Devotion*, III, 105–110.

"My poor boy, what will become of you?" This reprimand triggered a transformation in the boy. Raymond "changed in an instant," as his mother later recalled. He was suddenly obedient to every word and became much calmer and more reasonable. Oftentimes he hid behind the closet, where a small domestic altar was situated with an image of the Mother of all Grace of Czenstochau. Worried again by this demeanor, his mother asked, "What is it, my son?" He cried and explained to her, "I was very sad. And I asked the Blessed Virgin what was to become of me. The Blessed Virgin appeared to me. She had two crowns in her hands, a white one and a red one. She looked at me with love and asked me, which one I would like to choose. The white one signified that I was to remain pure, the red one that I was to die as a martyr. Whereupon, I answered the Holy Virgin, 'I choose both!' She smiled and disappeared..." As a good psychologist, his mother answered, "His radical change showed that the child spoke the truth!"

After a mission by the Franciscans, Franz and Raymond were promised a spot in the Franciscan seminary in Lemberg. Raymond was very gifted in practical things. He was passionate about mathematics and grew to be admired by his fellow pupils. He was a "horror" to his teachers because he asked complicated questions, not out of malice but out of interest. Quickly it became clear that he had a skill for inventing things. He enjoyed calculating interplanetary flights and he boasted before his amazed friends that he would one day construct an apparatus that would fly to the moon. Military and strategic plans were especially fascinating to him. This plunged him into a deep crisis of soul shortly before he wanted to enter the Order at the age of 16. He dreamed of becoming both a Polish soldier and a knight of his heavenly Mother. On his way to the Provincial Superior to say his farewell, he was called into the visitor's room of the school. His mother was waiting for him and joyfully told him her good news: Josef, his third brother, had also decided to enter the monastery. Their father had remained in Cracow with the Franciscans; she had traveled to Lemberg in order to join the Benedictine sisters. The whole family would be consecrated to God.

This news was like a thunderbolt for Raymond. He acknowledged the temptation which was keeping him from the consecrated life. On September 11, 1911, at the age of 17, he made his religious vows as Frater Maximilian Kolbe. He wished to become a Franciscan monk because this order has a special link to Blessed Duns Scotus and the teaching of the Immaculate Conception, and it seemed to him the most Marian of all. He wanted to belong entirely to Mary, since he owed everything to her, including his vocation. His childlike trust in Mary is especially interesting. He was not afraid to call Mary, "Mamma": "Be eternally blessed, Queen and Mistress, my dear mamma; you think of me, even though I am so full of pride and self-love. On Judgment Day, all will know that it was you who gave me everything, what I am and what I have. I myself am nothing. Be eternally blessed, O Immaculate! I am totally and absolutely yours, body and soul. My whole life, my death, and my eternal fate are yours. Do with me what you will. If you wish, take me right at this moment. If not, then later. Mommy, I am all yours." He liked to advise others: "See the Immaculate as if she were your mother. Do not worry about anything, just about her!"

Since Maximilian's superiors were aware of his skills, they sent him to study in Rome. He studied there until 1919. During that time he was taken ill with tuberculosis of the lungs. This became evident only later, when, after the First World War erupted, he spat up blood. Even though Maximilian expected to die quickly, he was filled with zeal and a fighting spirit. To celebrate the two-hundredth anniversary of the founding of Freemasonry in 1917, Rome was chosen as a place for sacrilegious mockery. Maximilian Kolbe personally witnessed the

Freemasons unraveling images of Satan under the windows of the Vatican, depicting the devil thrusting the Archangel Michael onto the ground. Underneath it read: "Satan has to rule the Vatican, the Pope will be his slave." On October 16, Maximilian fought back. He founded the *Militia Immaculatae*, the "Knights of the Immaculata". The most important aspect in the program of the Knights of the Immaculata was that the members fought for self-sanctification, the conversion of sinners, bring heretics back into the Catholic Church, defending the Church against Freemasonry, and spreading the devotion of the Miraculous Medal—their "ammunition," as Maximilian called it. All of this under the protection and with the help of Mary Immaculate! Consecration to Mary was the center of this Marian spirituality. Maximilian lived and renewed it day by day, even by small gestures, which showed his love for the Immaculate. At the end of each day before he went to sleep, he put his watch and his glasses at the feet of a small statue of the Madonna in his room, to show that all his time and all his skills belonged to Mary.

On April 28, 1918, he was ordained a priest in Rome. He celebrated his first Holy Mass in the Church of Sant'Andrea delle Frate, where the Immaculate Conception had appeared to the Jewish convert Alphons Maria Ratisbone. In July 1919 the young priest, still critically ill, returned to Poland. The doctors told him that he had only three months left to live. Nevertheless, he began to lecture as a professor in Cracow with a little more than a quarter of his lung! In order to reach the members of the "Knights," Maximilian published the small newspaper, *Knights of the Immaculata*, in 1922. There was no money to print additional copies, but the Mary Immaculate miraculously took care of that herself. Since the older brothers complained about the noise that was a result of the printing and mailing of the newest editions, Fr. Maximilian was moved to the monastery of Grodno.

The publication reached 30,000 copies in 1925. Around this time, Maximilian had to enter a sanatorium for eighteen months due to overexertion and a hemorrhage. Upon his return, the monastery of Grodno was overflowing with new brothers who wanted to join in order to help with the publication. The only solution to the lack of space was a new establishment. There was a place available near Warsaw; only money was lacking. Fr. Maximilian began by putting up a Marian statue and bartered for a price. The Provincial refused to pay the high sum. In obedience, the priest told Prince Drucki-Lubecki that the Order could not buy the property. "What should be done with the statue?" the Prince asked. Fr. Maximilian answered, "It can remain there." After reflecting, the prince then said, "Well, take the estate; I'll give it to you!" This was the beginning of the new "City of the Immaculata" (Niepokalanów). The numbers of the *Knights of the Immaculata* magazine grew year by year until it reached one million in 1939 when the Wehrmacht invaded. At the end, six priests and more than seven hundred brothers had worked in this monastery. From the years 1930 to 1936, Fr. Maximilian was able to publish his newspaper in Japan and India. In 1936, he took full responsibility of the Niepokalanów once again.

Maximilian Kolbe has given theology an important contribution, which might seem complicated at first glance. Maximilian asked himself, "Who are you, O Holy Mother?" In response, he recalled the words of the Mother of God at Lourdes, "I am the Immaculate Conception." Mary did not present herself as "Immaculately Conceived," but explicitly used the unusual and linguistically direct phrasing, "I am the Immaculate Conception." What did this mean? Maximilian Kolbe explained this sentence with regard to the Holy Trinity. God is Love. The Father loves the Son, and the Son loves the Father; the love between both of them is the Holy Spirit, and so He is the love personified. The Father begets the Son, and the Father and the Son breathe the Holy Spirit. The inner-divine processions distinguish the three Persons and put them in relation to one another. The Holy Spirit proceeds from the Father and the Son. It is He, according to Maximilian Kolbe, who is the eternally Immaculate Conception, the "fruit of Love" between the Father and the Son. The Holy Spirit, true God, as Father and Son, owes His being to the two Divine persons and does not bring forth another. In Mary, the Holy Spirit causes the greatest miracle: the Incarnation of God. In Mary, He is revealed in an outstanding manner, in and through His bride. Mary, as a creature, mirrors the fullness of grace, which she has received from God, and which defines the Divine Person of the Holy Spirit: conception. Nonetheless, there is an eternal distance between God and creature, but love and grace unite the Virgin Mary in an exceptional manner to the Holy Spirit. She is immaculate, without sin— that is, without obstacle for His effects. She is the created mirror, without stain or blemish, in which the increased light is reflected. She is an icon of the Holy Spirit painted by God Himself, who makes the invisible visible to men. She is the moon, that, in the night of sin, casts the light of the sun upon the earth. She is the Immaculate Conception and gives, as an aqueduct channels water, everything that she has received from God to others, without any self-love or vanity. She mediates His grace.

On February 17, 1941, Maximilian was seized by the Gestapo and deported to Auschwitz. After being beaten by one of the guards for his faith, he was transferred to the sickbed. Just slightly recovered, he was moved to Block 14. On one evening, in July of 1941, one of the prisoners fled from the block and could not be captured. As a punishment ten prisoners were chosen for execution. One of them was Franz Gajowniczek, the father of a family. Father Kolbe stepped out of line and said to the camp commander, "I am a Catholic priest. I want to take the spot of this man, since he has a wife and children." This exchange was granted. The ten prisoners were taken to the starvation bunker. Here, Fr. Maximilian encouraged his fellow suffering brothers, chanted Marian hymns, and helped them to prepare for death. On August 14, 1941, the day before the feast of the Assumption of Mary into heaven, a nurse entered the death-bunker and killed the remaining four prisoners by lethal injection. The last of the ten was Fr. Maximilian Kolbe. Shortly before his imprisonment, Fr. Maximilian explained to his brothers, "With the help of the Immaculate, we are capable of accomplishing every heroic act, just as she would have done in our place. Especially in order to love God, as she loves Him, with her own heart... that is something we can only learn on our knees!"

As his body was burned on August 15, 1941, his desire was fulfilled: "I want and wish to be crushed to dust for the cause of the Immaculate and God. May the wind carry this dust into the world, so that nothing of me may remain. Only then will my sacrifice to the Immaculate be complete."

Prayer of St. Maximilan Kolbe

Allow me to praise You, O most holy Virgin Mary. Allow me to praise You with my personal commitment and sacrifice. Allow me to live, work, suffer, be consumed, and die for You, only for You. Allow me to bring the whole world to You. Allow me to contribute to your ever-greater exaltation, to Your greatest possible exaltation. Allow me to give You such glory that no one else has ever given until now. Allow others to surpass me in zeal for Your exaltation and for me to surpass them, so that by means of such noble rivalry, Your glory may increase ever more profoundly, ever more rapidly, ever more intensely as He, Who has exalted You so indescribably above all other beings, Himself desires. Amen.

Mary—The Humble Virgin

Invocation of the Holy Spirit

Breathe in me, O Holy Spirit,
that my thoughts may all be holy.
Act in me, O Holy Spirit,
that my work, too, may be holy.
Draw my heart, O Holy Spirit,
that I love but what is holy.
Strengthen me, O Holy Spirit,
to defend all that is holy.
Guard me, then, O Holy Spirit,
that I always may be holy. Amen.

(St. Augustine)

Scripture Reading

The Annunciation

Luke 1:26-38

In the sixth month the angel Gabriel was sent from God to
a city of Galilee named Nazareth, to a virgin betrothed to a
man whose name was Joseph, of the house of David. And

the virgin's name was Mary. And he came to her and said, "Greetings, O favored one, the Lord is with you!" But she was greatly troubled at the saying, and tried to discern what sort of greeting this might be. And the angel said to her, "Do not be afraid, Mary, for you have found favor with God. And behold, you will conceive in your womb and bear a son, and you shall call his name Jesus. He will be great and will be called the Son of the Most High. And the Lord God will give to him the throne of his father David, and he will reign over the house of Jacob forever, and of his kingdom there will be no end." And Mary said to the angel, "How will this be, since I am a virgin?" And the angel answered her, "The Holy Spirit will come upon you, and the power of the Most High will overshadow you; therefore the child to be born will be called holy—the Son of God. And behold, your relative Elizabeth in her old age has also conceived a son, and this is the sixth month with her who was called barren. For nothing will be impossible with God." And Mary said, "Behold, I am the servant of the Lord; let it be to me according to your word." And the angel departed from her.

Reflection

From the expulsion from Paradise and the prophecy of the coming Savior, all men were in expectation of salvation. All of Israel waited yearningly for the foretold Messiah, who was anticipated as a shining hero who would cast all enemies of the Jews from their land. Mary also longingly expected the liberator of Israel and undoubtedly prayed constantly for His coming. God heard her prayer, as she probably would have never expected it. Already in her Immaculate Conception He had prepared her, that she might be a worthy home for the Eternal Word. That is why the angel calls her, "full of grace": she is a pure vessel, filled with God's grace! Nothing sin-like, nor anything displeasing to God could be found in her. Mary, the humble handmaid, is taken aback at this greeting.

Through Gabriel, His messenger, God communicates the question to Mary to become the Mother of Jesus. Let us imagine how all of heaven holds its breath at this moment! The salvation of the whole world depends on the "Yes" of this young girl, because God respects human freedom and His dignity to such an extent that He asks Mary to become His mother.

Mary wants to obey God, but she hesitates to say, "Yes," since she had vowed to live a chaste and virgin life, even though she was engaged to Joseph. Were it not so, she would not have asked how the conception could take place. The angel encourages Mary, since Christ would not have a human father, but the Holy Spirit would cause His incarnation in the womb of the Blessed Virgin Mother. Dedicating her whole heart, she answered, "Let it be done to me according to Your word!" In this very moment, the Eternal Word, the infinite God, becomes man in the Virgin Mary. The Incarnation of God, who for our salvation did not hesitate to leave the glory of heaven and become a tiny, defenseless human being in the womb of His holy mother, let this hour in Nazareth be the beginning of our salvation. For the Blessed Virgin Mary, this might have been the most overjoyed moment of her life. God became a child; her creator became her son!

We can admire this great mystery and rejoice. Let us ask the Mother of God that we may receive every Holy Communion with as much love as she had received Christ in this blessed hour in Nazareth.

Decade of the Rosary

The first Joyful Mystery: the Annunciation of the Lord
We thank God that He chose Mary as His mother and became man for our salvation.

Prayer to the Mother of God

Hail, O Star of the ocean,
God's own Mother blest,
ever sinless Virgin,
gate of heav'nly rest.

Taking that sweet Ave,
which from Gabriel came,
peace confirm within us,
changing Eve's name."[6]

Break the sinners' fetters,
make our blindness day,
Chase all evils from us,
for all blessings pray.

Show thyself a Mother,
may the Word divine
born for us thine Infant
hear our prayers through thine.

Virgin all excelling,
mildest of the mild,
free from guilt preserve us
meek and undefiled.

Keep our life all spotless,
make our way secure
till we find in Jesus,
joy for evermore.

---

6. Play on words: AVE—EVA; Eve brought death, and Mary brought life
   when she gave her "yes" to the angel!

Praise to God the Father,
honor to the Son,
in the Holy Spirit,
be the glory one. Amen.

Closing Prayer

Holy God, Your Eternal Word was made flesh in the womb of the Blessed Virgin Mary, as the Angel had proclaimed. Therefore, we praise her as the Mother of God. Hear her intercession, and grant all people salvation in Jesus Christ, Your Son, Our Lord and God, in the unity of the Holy Spirit, who lives and reigns with You for ever and ever. Amen.

Spiritual Reading

Mary, Mediatrix of all Graces

Mary is daughter, mother and bride of God. God loves her more than all other creatures, because she loves him more than all others. That is why God lets her participate in his glory in extraordinary fashion. The blessed Virgin can distribute his graces; she is the treasure chest, his channel, by which he wants to pour blessings forth upon all men. We can rejoice in this beauty and the power of Mary and thank God with all our hearts for such a woman. Let us ask him, that we may love her, as He loves her!

From the *Treatise on True Devotion*

God the Father gathered all the waters together and called them the seas (Maria). He gathered all his graces together and called them Mary (Maria). The great God has a treasury or storehouse full of riches in which he has enclosed all that is beautiful, resplendent, rare, and precious, even his own Son.

This immense treasury is none other than Mary whom the saints call the "treasury of the Lord". From her fullness all men are made rich.

God the Son imparted to his mother all that he gained by his life and death, namely, his infinite merits and his eminent virtues. He made her the treasurer of all his Father had given him as heritage. Through her he applies his merits to his members and through her he transmits his virtues and distributes his graces. She is his mystical channel, his aqueduct, through which he causes his mercies to flow gently and abundantly.

God the Holy Spirit entrusted his wondrous gifts to Mary, his faithful spouse, and chose her as the dispenser of all he possesses, so that she distributes all his gifts and graces to whom she wills, as much as she wills, how she wills and when she wills. No heavenly gift is given to men who does not pass through her virginal hands. Such indeed is the will of God, who has decreed that we should have all things through Mary, so that, making herself poor and lowly,, and hiding herself in the depths of nothingness during her whole life, she might be enriched, exalted and honored by almighty God. Such are the views of the Church and the early Fathers.[7]

From the Lives of the Saints

Saint Louis-Marie Grignion de Montfort

On January 31, 1673, St. Louis-Marie Grignion was born in Montfort in Brittany, France. During his time at school with the Jesuits, he decided to become a priest. He wanted to become a holy priest who would live for love of Christ, one who would live a poor life and save many souls. With no belongings, he left his home for Paris with a joyful and free heart: "It is finished; I move about in the world, I am

---

7. *True Devotion*, I, 23–25.

as a vagabond." His money and best suit were given to the homeless.

During his studies in Paris, Louis encountered much resistance. The Church in France, which was led by many Jansenist bishops, was in danger of falling into heresy. The Jansenists did not speak about the merciful love of God, but believed that only those whom God had predestined could be saved. As a result, the general populace lived either an exaggerated penance, or, as was the case for the majority, an indifference to faith. In the end, what sense is there in living a good life if God is so merciless and had already chosen a few good men?

St. Louis knew that God wanted to save all men and had provided them with the necessary means for salvation in order to reach heaven. Already in 1700, the year of his priestly ordination, he wrote: "When I see the misery of the Church, I can do nothing but plea for a small society of priests to go from parish to parish under the banner and protection of the Blessed Virgin Mary and preach the Gospel to the poor, relying only on God's providence (that is, without payment)." Years later, he founded the "Society of Mary," which had the aim of living this very ideal.

Louis-Marie became a great missionary of the people, preaching through the land. His success among the simple was not met with joy by every bishop. Time and again, he had to flee from the Jansenist shepherds and begin his apostolate from scratch. In seven dioceses he was even forbidden from evangelizing at all! After six years of grueling work, he asked himself if he could truly carry out God's will and decided to ask the Pope for guidance: "I believe in the word of the Holy Father. He is my head and my light. I do not see what is before my eyes; he sees everything clearly." The response of Pope Clement XI was brief and precise: "Dear Sir, in France you have a great enough area for your zeal. Do not go anywhere else."

With renewed strength, St. Louis returned from Rome: he preached unceasingly, composed religious hymns, which were soon sung by women and children on the streets, he put up wayside crosses, and, of course, he prayed often. Through the night he besought God for the conversion of his country.

Among his countless writings,—his works fill over 18,000 pages!—*True Devotion to Mary*, published years after his death in 1842, is the most significant. This book is regarded as one of the most beautiful books about Marian devotion and a guide to the renewal of one's baptismal vows and the associated consecration to Jesus through Mary. The life program of St. Louis is rather simple: "Through Mary, Christ came into this world; through Mary, He also wants to rule the world!" The consecration to Mary, which Grignion teaches, is nothing new. In fact, it is ancient and deeply rooted in Church Tradition. It is the "royal way" of following Christ, which countless saints have treaded over the centuries.

For the eighteenth century, the preaching of St. Louis was an important inspiration of renewal and repentance. To this day, the importance of this saint, whose writings have been translated into more than 200 languages, has not ceased.

Louis-Marie wanted to be a saintly man of God and to preach the Gospel with burning zeal. In his prayers, he begged the Apostles to make him as themselves: "What do we ask of You? Nothing for ourselves—all for Your glory. We pray to You for holy priests. For priests who can, without earthly worries or ties, without thirst for power or obstinacy, foster the wish to educate helpers for the kingdom of God. They should always stand guard for You and always be ready to obey You. May they be true children of Mary, filled with the same Spirit that filled the Holy Virgin. With Your good news on their lips, and Mary's Rosary in hand, they must be blazing fires, brilliant stars that lighten the darkness of the world. May their love for Mary be fully internal and constant; truly internal, but at the same time, a source of strength for great deeds. Should no one come to defend You, almighty God? Should there be no fighters for Your cause and banner? Let us be crying voices, Lord, which proclaims the call to arms everywhere! To fight for the kingdom of God! O Lord, make for Yourself an army of apostles, a royal guard. They will protect Your dwelling place, protect Your honor, and save souls, so that there will be only one shepherd and one flock, and all men will praise You in Your temple! Amen."

Throughout his whole life, St. Louis-Marie exhibited a great love for the sick and the poor. When one night he found a pariah on the street, he carried him home on his shoulders. He insistently knocked at the door and said, "Open for Christ!" Then he laid the sick man on his own bed and cared for him as well as he could. Another time, when he was already a preacher of note, he secretly entered a monastery of nuns and begged for a donation: "Alms for the love of God!" He was refused. The next day, he made another attempt, but this time he revealed his identity. Immediately, the sisters received him, apologized repeatedly, and served him abundantly. But St. Louis strongly reprimanded them, "Now I receive everything in abundance, but the one who asked only for a piece of bread in Jesus' name you sent away. That is not a lack of love, but also of faith!"

He died at the age of forty-three during a mission to the people in St-Laurent-sur-Sèvre on April 28, 1716. His motto was *God alone!* At the time of his death, his community of missionaries totaled two priests and four lay brothers. Today, they number approximately 2,000.

Prayer of St. Louis-Marie Grignion de Montfort

O admirable Mother, present me to your dear Son as His eternal slave, so that as He has redeemed me by you, by you He may receive me!

O Mother of Mercy, grant me the grace to obtain the true Wisdom of God, and for that end receive me among those whom you love and teach, whom you lead, nourish and protect as your children and your slaves.

O faithful Virgin, make me in all things so perfect a disciple, imitator and slave of the Incarnate Wisdom, Jesus Christ your Son, that I may attain, by your intercession and by your example, to the fullness of His age on earth and of His glory in Heaven. Amen.

THIRD DAY

Mary—Everlasting Counsel

Invocation of the Holy Spirit

Breathe in me, O Holy Spirit,
that my thoughts may all be holy.
Act in me, O Holy Spirit,
that my work, too, may be holy.
Draw my heart, O Holy Spirit,
that I love but what is holy.
Strengthen me,
O Holy Spirit, to defend all that is holy.
Guard me, then, O Holy Spirit,
that I always may be holy. Amen.

(St. Augustine)

Scripture Reading

The Visitation

Luke 1:39-48

In those days Mary arose and went with haste into the hill
country, to a town in Judah, and she entered the house of
Zechariah and greeted Elizabeth. And when Elizabeth heard
the greeting of Mary, the baby leaped in her womb. And

Elizabeth was filled with the Holy Spirit, and she exclaimed with a loud cry, "Blessed are you among women, and blessed is the fruit of your womb! And why is this granted to me that the mother of my Lord should come to me? For behold, when the sound of your greeting came to my ears, the baby in my womb leaped for joy. And blessed is she who believed that there would be a fulfillment of what was spoken to her from the Lord." And Mary said, "My soul magnifies the Lord, and my spirit rejoices in God my Savior, for he has looked on the humble estate of his servant. For behold, from now on all generations will call me blessed.

Reflection

What a joy it must have been for Mary, to become the Mother of God! She feels an inner urge to hasten to Elizabeth, who, as the angel had promised her, is expecting a child and in need of her aid. Mary willingly takes the long way, to assist her relative. Because of this, Christ travels in her womb through the land of his people for the first time. That is why Mary is called: the Ark of the Covenant. Just as the ark, which king David had brought into the Temple of Jerusalem, was the throne of God, so too Mary is His throne in a much more perfect sense: she carries the God-Man, the Savior of Israel in her womb! Until today it remains the mission of the Mother of God to be the bearer of Christ. Therefore in many pictures Mary is depicted holding Christ. She is like a candelabrum bearing the true light, wanting it to shine upon all men. Mary only desires to bring Jesus to all men. Whoever calls to Mary for help, honoring her and consecrating himself to her, can be sure that she will draw him closer to Christ. Mary and Jesus are inseparable! Where the Mother is there too is the Son!

Because the Mother of God made the long journey through the mountains to help her relative Elizabeth with the birth of St. John, we call Mary the Perpetual Help. The essence of her being is devotion and her duty to help. She calls herself the: "handmaid of the Lord." From her we can learn the true spirit of charity: to hasten to help our neighbor; to give without measure; to offer oneself without the expectation of repayment!

Elizabeth rejoices upon Mary's arrival, as she is especially needy in the last weeks before the birth. Even more she is gladdened by her relative's visit, since through the revelation of the Holy Spirit she has become aware that Mary is the mother of the Messiah. She is the first devotee of Mary, who says joyfully: "Blessed art though amongst women!" And to this day her words have not been silenced, as we pray them in every Hail Mary. The Mother of God does not refuse this honor, since she is aware that her praise will be incessant. She realizes that the greeting of St. Elisabeth is the beginning of the devotion to Mary, which will endure from generation to generation: "For behold, from now on all generations will call me blessed!" But Mary remains the humble handmaid. She accepts the greeting of her relative and transforms it into a glorious praise of God, who had done great things for her. At every moment, when we honor Mary, she takes our joyful prayer and transforms it into a praise of her Son, who she carries in her heart always.

Decade of the Rosary

The second Joyful Mystery: The Visitation of the Blessed Virgin Mary to her cousin Elizabeth

With every Hail Mary, let us join the praise of St. Elizabeth and be thankful for the Perpetual Help of Mary.

Prayer to the Mother of God (Memorare)

Remember, O most gracious Virgin Mary, that never was it known that anyone who fled to Your protection, implored Your help, or sought Your intercession was left unaided. Inspired by this confidence, I fly unto You, O Virgin of virgins, my mother; to You do I come, before You I stand, sinful and sorrowful. O Mother of the Word Incarnate, despise not my petitions, but in Your mercy hear and answer me. Amen.

Closing Prayer

God, You are Redeemer of all men. Through the Blessed Virgin Mary, the Arc of the new Covenant, You brought joy and peace to the house of Elisabeth. Let us follow the inspiration of Your Spirit, that we may also bring Christ to our brothers and that we may glorify You by our worship and our holy life. We ask this through Jesus Christ, Your Son, our Lord and God, in the unity of the Holy Spirit, who lives and reigns with You forever and ever. Amen.

Spiritual Reading

A complete consecration to Mary

When we call ourselves "Christians," we already express that the greatest goal of our life is, to becomes ever more like Christ, that we may be worthy of carrying his name. Since Mary without doubt resembles Christ more than any creature, we can learn under her guidance, what it means, to follow Jesus. Everything that we give to her will make us more like her son. We would be stupid, if we would not let our devotion to Mary be a complete one and if we wanted to keep something from this good mother. Everything should be hers, so that she—as mothers do for their children—cares, saves, refines and perfects it, to give it to Christ, thereupon.

From the *Treatise on True Devotion*

As all perfection consists in our being conformed, united and consecrated to Jesus it naturally follows that the most perfect of all devotions is that which conforms, unites, and consecrates us most completely to Jesus. Now of all God's creatures Mary is the most conformed to Jesus. It therefore follows that, of all devotions, devotion to her makes for the most effective consecration and conformity to him. The more one is consecrated to Mary, the more one is consecrated to Jesus.

That is why perfect consecration to Jesus is but a perfect and complete consecration of oneself to the Blessed Virgin, which is the devotion I teach; or in other words, it is the perfect renewal of the vows and promises of holy baptism.

This devotion consists in giving oneself entirely to Mary in order to belong entirely to Jesus through her. It requires us to give:

(1) Our body with its senses and members;

(2) Our soul with its faculties;

(3) Our present material possessions and all we shall acquire in the future;

(4) Our interior and spiritual possessions, that is, our merits, virtues and good actions of the past, the present and the future.

In other words, we give her all that we possess both in our natural life and in our spiritual life as well as everything we shall acquire in the future in the order of nature, of grace, and of glory in heaven. This we do without any reservation, not even of a penny, a hair, or the smallest good deed. And we give for all eternity without claiming or expecting, in return for our offering and our service, any other reward than the honor of belonging to our Lord through Mary and in Mary, even though our Mother were not—as in fact she always is—the most generous and appreciative of all God's creatures.[8]

From the Lives of the Saints

St. Bernadette Soubirous

On September 22, 1909, Bernadette Soubirous' grave was opened thirty years after her death. The body was found without any sign of decay, while the shroud was decomposed and the cross was rusted. Incorrupt as she was found, today she rests in a gold and crystal sarcophagus in the Chapel of the Monastery of Nevers.

Bernadette did not have the tendency to create illusions and lively fantasies, nor did she have a need for recognition. She was illiterate, and at the age of fourteen she barely managed to learn the Hail Mary to at least be able to pray the Rosary. With her impoverished parents she lived in a dark cell of a former prison of Lourdes. The walls were damp and mold spread through the cracks in the wall; no rays of sunlight warmed this home. Living in this environment, Bernadette fell ill with asthma. During the long nights she would press her forehead against the iron grid of the windows so as not to suffocate. Despite sickness, poverty, cold and hunger, she never lost her natural joy. She experienced happy days when she was able to watch the sheep of a well natured farmer's lady and could eat a full meal. On dark winter evenings, Bernadette led her family in praying the Rosary at home.

Bernadette would have loved to receive First Communion. But even at the age of fourteen she was considered too sim-

---

8. *True Devotion*, IV, 120–121.

ple-minded, as she could not remember the questions and answers of the Catechism. Miracles and visions were even more foreign to her.

Then came February 11, 1858. Bernadette was on the shore of the Gave collecting wood. She had just taken off her cold wooden shoes and her socks in order to wade through the water. It was then that suddenly, above a wild rose bush in a grotto on the other side of a rock, Massabiell, she saw a young lady with a blue-lined white mantle. A veil rested on her head and from her right arm hung a white Rosary. With a smile, the woman invited Bernadette to come near. Over the next fourteen days, Bernadette saw the same vision every day. The lady promised to make her happy, not in this life, but surely in the next. Then she asked that Bernadette pray for sinners and that she have a chapel built by the parish priest on the site of the apparition, where processions and pilgrimages should be made.

Against her will, she was compelled by her parents and friends to tell of her experiences. Her friends made fun of her, calling her names, and her mother wanted to punish her. Bernadette had to receive permission from her parents to go to the grotto again. Parents and neighbors followed her to the site. Together they prayed the Rosary up to the point of Bernadette falling into ecstasy. She spoke to an invisible figure, moved closer to the rock with a smile, and did not even feel the flame of a candle, which burned through her hand. Dr. Sozous, a freethinking agnostic accompanied them to prove that she was a liar. However, he examined her and found a pulse in her hand. Over the following days more and more people came. The mayor tried to forbid people from visiting the Grotto. The parish priest of Lourdes reproached Bernadette strongly and refused to follow the instructions of the vision because the Lady had not uttered her name. It was only after Bernadette dug into the ground as the Lady had told her to do, and exposed a miraculous source of water which could heal the sick, that Mary revealed her name on March 25: "I am the Immaculate Conception." The parish priest revered the miracle that God had performed in his village. Henceforth, he became the most solicitous guardian of the child, whom the prefect of Tarbes wanted to have thrown into an asylum.

Bernadette remained as she was: a nice, humble child with a natural wit. Further, she attended her catechism class twice a day in order to prepare for her First Communion. She called some irrational forms of veneration "stupidity!" In July of 1860, she helped in the hospice of Lourdes in the kitchen and in the garden. In this way, she was somewhat protected from the people, but not from the countless questions of the bishop's investigating committee, which monitored and examined the case for more than four years before they admitted: "In God's holy name! We believe that the Immaculate Mother of God did appear to the girl, Bernadette Soubirous."

The Bishop of Nevers arranged for her acceptance into a monastery. The nuns expected a well-educated girl but found in her a simplicity of heart. They made her feel their low esteem of her. The superiors spared her no humiliations, with the pretext of preventing the visionary of Lourdes from becoming prideful. Bernadette would have probably remained a novice until the end of her life, had she not fallen sick with a terminal illness. In this state, no one could have denied her the opportunity of professing her vows. To this girl, who was humiliated for thirteen years because of her visions, God gave the strength to say: "See, my story is very simple: the Virgin made me serve her, then I was put in the corner. This is my place now. I am happy here, and I will remain here."

Her end drew near at the beginning of the year 1879. In addition to her asthma, she suffered from rheumatism, coughing up of blood, and a heart condition, while creeping tuberculosis of the bones consigned her to bed. She died after long, difficult death on April 16, 1879. Her last humble prayer was, "Holy Mary, Mother of God, pray for me a poor sinner, a poor sinner, a poor sinner!"

Bernadette Soubirous was canonized by Pope Pius XI on December 8, 1933. Her visions of the Virgin Mary, which we celebrate each year on February 11, are a confirmation from Heaven for the dogma of the Immaculate Conception, which was proclaimed in 1854. The countless miraculous cures of Lourdes, which even today astound believers and agnostic scientists, are proof of the power and the greatness of Mary.

Prayer of St. Bernadette

O Mary, my good Mother,
Help me follow your example to be generous in every sacrifice that Our Lord may ask of me during my life.
O Mother, offer me to Jesus.
Take my heart and unite it with the heart of my Jesus.

FOURTH DAY

Mary—Mother of God

Invocation of the Holy Spirit

Breathe in me, O Holy Spirit,
that my thoughts may all be holy.
Act in me, O Holy Spirit,
that my work, too, may be holy.
Draw my heart, O Holy Spirit,
that I love but what is holy.
Strengthen me, O Holy Spirit,
to defend all that is holy.
Guard me, then, O Holy Spirit,
that I always may be holy. Amen.

(St. Augustine)

Scripture Reading

The Nativity of Christ

Luke 2, 1-7

In those days a decree went out from Caesar Augustus that all
the world should be registered. This was the first registration
when Quirinius was governor of Syria. And all went to be

registered, each to his own town. And Joseph also went up
from Galilee, from the town of Nazareth, to Judea, to the
city of David, which is called Bethlehem, because he was of
the house and lineage of David, to be registered with Mary,
his betrothed, who was with child. And while they were there,
the time came for her to give birth. And she gave birth to her
firstborn son and wrapped him in swaddling cloths and laid
him in a manger, because there was no place for them in the
inn.

Reflection

The prophecy of prophet Micah that the Messiah would
be born in Bethlehem is centuries old. God uses the state
authority: it was because of Emperor Augustus' census that
Mary and Joseph needed to wander to Bethlehem in order to
fulfill the prophecy. The birth of Jesus is therefore one of the
examples of how God has guided and prepared everything in
His providence: even a pagan Emperor serves the purpose of
Divine will!

Mary is full of trust in Divine providence and willingly
makes her burdensome way to Bethlehem. She endures the
rejection of the overcrowded inns and is grateful for shelter
in a poor stable. Surely she suffered for the fact that her Son
had to lie in a hard manger and that she could barely protect
him from the cold wind. Nevertheless, she was overjoyed in
that hour: without pain she bore the world the Savior, the
Redeemer and Savior! His birth, which was not touched by
original sin, did not weaken or hurt His mother. She was the
first one to fall on her knees in adoration before the manger,
in which God lay as a helpless Child. He smiles to His mother
and to all who came after her in prayer up to our present day.
The Divine Child extends His hands to all of them.

Soon the shepherds arrived, the humble examples of true Christian love; they came to the manger to adore the divine Infant. They did not find the silk and satin of a prince, but an inconspicuous newborn infant, wrapped in swaddling clothes, as the angel had promised. The humble shepherds believed nonetheless and fell to their knees in adoration. Mary held the child Jesus up to them so that they might see and caress Him. In this hour, the shepherds recognized their Messiah and His holy mother, who reveals herself to them as Mediatrix of all graces. It is she who brought the divine child to them, who gave the Savior to the world and who wanted to show Jesus to all men, that He be venerated and loved by all people. Just as Christ wanted to come to the world through Mary, so too does He wish to be venerated and honored through her. Let us go humbly to the Mother of God, as the shepherds did, that she may show us Jesus. Bethlehem translated means "house of bread." There, the true bread, which has come down from Heaven, becomes visible. Jesus, who lies in the manger, will, at the end of His life, give Himself to His own as food and drink in the mystery of the Eucharist. The Divine Child in swaddling clothes will make Himself even smaller and more humble, when He lies on our altars in the species of bread. Let us ask Jesus that we may recognize Him in the inconspicuous appearance of the holy host, and as Mary did we prepare our hearts as mangers for Him.

Decade of the Rosary

The third Joyful Mystery: The Birth of Jesus of the Blessed Virgin Mary in the stable at Bethlehem

With the shepherds and St. Joseph let us kneel down in the stable and marvel at how humble almighty God is, who lies in a manger.

Prayer to the Mother of God (Alma Redemptoris Mater)

Star of sea and ocean,
Gateway to God's haven,
Mother of our Maker,
Hear our prayer, O Maiden.

Welcoming the Ave,
Gabriel's simple greeting,
You have borne a Savior
Far beyond all dreaming.

Loose the bonds that hold us
Bound in sin's own blindness
That with eyes now opened
God's own light may guide us.

Show yourself our mother;
He will hear your pleading
Whom your womb has sheltered
And whose hand brings healing.

Gentlest of all virgins,
That our love be faithful
Keep us from all evil,
Gentle, strong, and grateful.

Guard us through life's dangers,
Never turn and leave us
May our hope find harbor
In the calm of Jesus.

Sing to God our Father
Through the Son who saves us,
Joyful in the Spirit,
Everlasting praises. Amen.

Closing Prayer

Almighty God, by the motherhood of the Blessed Virgin Mary, You have given eternal salvation to us. Hasten to help us through the intercession of Your humble Handmaid, who has given us the creator of life, Jesus Christ, Your Son, our Lord and God, who reigns with you in the Holy Spirit, one God forever and ever. Amen.

Spiritual Reading

The consecration to Mary as a renewal of Baptismal Promises

St. Louis-Marie Grignion is convinced that the lukewarmness of so many Christians is caused by a negligence of their baptismal promises. The consecration to Mary is supposed to be a renewed renunciation of the devil and of sin, a conscious giving of oneself to Christ through the hands of his mother. Therefore the consecration to Mary requires a conscious decision for the faith and a radical change of life. All shall belong to God. We need not be afraid of this full devotion or even fear personal disadvantage, since Jesus and Mary will never be surpassed in magnanimity and kindness.

From the *Treatise on True Devotion*

I have said that this devotion could rightly be called a perfect renewal of the vows and promises of holy baptism. Before baptism every Christian was a slave of the devil because he belonged to him. At baptism he has either personally or through his sponsors solemnly renounced Satan, his seductions and his works. He has chosen Jesus as his Master and sovereign Lord and undertaken to depend upon him as a slave of love. This is what is done in the devotion I am presenting to you.

We renounce the devil, the world, sin and self, as expressed in the act of consecration, and we give ourselves entirely to Jesus through Mary. We even do something more than at baptism, when ordinarily our god-parents speak for us and we are given to Jesus only by proxy. In this devotion we give ourselves personally and freely and we are fully aware of what we are doing.

In holy baptism we do not give ourselves to Jesus explicitly through Mary, nor do we give him the value of our good actions. After Baptism we remain entirely free either to apply that value to anyone we wish or keep it for ourselves. But by this consecration we give ourselves explicitly to Jesus through Mary's hands and we include in our consecration the value of all our actions.

Some may object that this devotion makes us powerless to help the souls of our relatives, friends and benefactors, since it requires us to give our Lord, through Mary, the value of our good works, prayers, penances, and alms-giving.

To that I reply: It is inconceivable that our friends, relatives and benefactors should suffer any loss because we have dedicated and consecrated ourselves unconditionally to the service of Jesus and Mary; it would be an affront to the power and goodness of Jesus and Mary who will surely come to the aid of our relatives, friends and benefactors whether from our meager spiritual assets or from other sources.

Secondly this devotion does not prevent us from praying for others, both the living and the dead, even though the application of our good works depends on the will of our Blessed Lady. On the contrary, it will make us pray with even greater confidence. Imagine a rich man, who, wanting to show his esteem for a great prince, gives his entire fortune to him. Would not that man have greater confidence in asking the prince to help one of his friends who needed assistance? Indeed the prince would only be too happy to have such an opportunity of proving his gratitude to one who had sacrificed all that he possessed to enrich him, thereby impoverishing himself to do him honor. The same must be said of our Lord and Our Lady. They will never allow themselves to be outdone in gratitude.[9]

From the Lives of the Saints

St. John Bosco

"John has become crazy! A priest cannot possibly act like that!" This must have been the reaction of the good people of Turin. Don Bosco oftentimes acted as a clown, a magician, or an acrobat. You could see him ropewalking, witness him making a coin disappear only to then pull it back out of someone's nose, or catch him spitting fire, as though he had worked for the circus. If it were not for his black cassock, then one might have thought he was a traveling showman who performed his tricks to make a living. His interest did not lie in the money of his fascinated young audience, but in their hearts, which he wished to win over for God. *"Da mihi animas, cetera tolle!"* This short Latin phrase, displayed in his office in Turin, was to become the life motto of Don Bosco and explained why John literally "stood on his own head," in order to get the children and young people off the streets: "Lord, give me souls, take from me everything else!"

John Bosco was born on August 16, 1815, not far from Turin. His father had died when he was still a young boy. His mother tried to manage the poor farm by herself. When he was nine-years-old, John had a visionary "dream," in which God prepared him for his later life's work.

In the vision, he saw a courtyard with children who were playing joyfully, but also cursing from time to time. John

---

9. *True Devotion*, IV, 131,132.

wanted to rush over to the ill-behaved boys to make them stop when, suddenly, a glorious man appeared. A white robe covered his whole silhouette. His face radiated with such power that one could not look at him. He told John that he needed to use kindness, not blows, to win over these children. John did not understand. The man said he would give him a teacher, and a majestic Lady showed up. She instructed John to watch, and the boys turned into wild animals—bears, goats, dogs, cats, and other creatures. "This," she told him, "is your field of work. Make yourself humble, strong, and energetic, so that you'll be able to do for my children what you'll see now." And the beasts turned into gentle lambs. In his confusion, John began to cry. The Lady assured him that in due time he would understand. And he woke up.

His oldest brother-in-law mocked him after having heard of the "dream," but his mother thought that John might become a priest. She would have loved John to study, but where would they find the means? John knew a way He would earn the money. No work was too dirty or too difficult for him. He patched straw hats, knit socks, and helped farmers in the fields. His early years were hard, but still joyful and pious. He was always surrounded by a group of boys. His authority was never challenged, because he made an impression on all. He could bend horseshoes with his bare hands, jump onto a galloping horse, perform magic tricks, ropewalk, and had mastered many trades; he was a person whom everyone wanted to emulate. But the reason was clear to him as to why he wanted to impress the children with his tricks, his strength, and expertise. He wanted to act as an apostle of Christ in order to conquer hearts for God: "Lord, give me souls, take from me everything else!" That was the reason he led his friends to church and prayed the Rosary with them.

In high school, his extraordinary memory and discipline in work helped him pass even with all of his time constraints, since he had to earn money on the side. It helped that he would sometimes dream about the course material of the tests beforehand. He could finally enter the seminary when he was twenty-years-old. A stipend helped him not to worry about finances. He studied, and followed a strict daily schedule. There was little time for sleep and recreation; most hours were given to books and manuals. Finally, he was ordained a priest.

In Turin, the young chaplain quickly realized how the youth in the streets were completely on their own. Countless numbers of homeless children roamed the city. Don Bosco knew what danger there was in such a life for boys if they grew up without support and education. That was another reason he performed his tricks: to gain the trust of the homeless boys. First they met on Sundays, and then Don Bosco started to build houses for his protégés. His kindness and his cordial goodwill to each of them helped him to win over the hearts of the children. With Don Bosco they had found a home in which they were sheltered and free at the same time, where they were loved and supported. Once, a priest friend visited Don Bosco and saw him playing with the boys and wondered if it was not too much chaos for him. "They can chop wood on my back as long as it keeps them from sinning," replied Don Bosco.

He repeatedly ran into problems with the authorities of the town, disappointments with the youngsters, and a lack of money. Yet, Don Bosco did not give up. He continued building house after house. Some of the older boys started to help him. From that sprang the "Salesian" Order, which aimed at continuing the youth-work heritage of Don Bosco. When someone wanted to praise him for his immense success, he would respond: "These people do not know who Don Bosco is. The one who does everything is Mary, Help of Christians."

His trust in Mary was so profound that he promised the boys that not a single one of them would be infected with cholera—which had claimed hundreds of victims—if they would only avoid sin, keep God's grace, and wear a Marian medal. Although many of his students volunteered in caring for those sick with the plague in the city hospitals, not one of them ever became ill.

The dreams and visions of St. Don Bosco are well known. Among the most famous is the one from 1862 in which he saw the adoration of the Eucharist and the true devotion to the Mother of God, that will save the Church: "Imagine we are on a seashore, or even better, on a lonely cliff, and there is no land underneath our feet. We can see countless ships on the ocean, which have organized themselves for a sea battle. They are equipped with naval rams, canons, muskets and other kinds of weapons and explosives. They all approach one vessel, which is much larger than they are, and try to damage it with their rams, try to set it on fire and cause it as much damage as possible. The large vessel is accompanied by smaller ships, which receive orders from it and defend the majestic ship against the oncoming fleet. The wind is against them and the rough sea seems to support the attackers. In the middle of the ocean there are two mighty pillars in close vicinity. One is crowned with a statue of Mary Immaculate, on whose base is inscribed: "Auxilium Christianorum" (Help of Christians). On the second much higher and mightier column there is a gigantic Host, along with the words: "Salus Credentium" (Salvation of the Faithful). The Pope, as the captain of the large ship, recognizes the rage of his enemies and the imminent danger that he and his people are in. He gathers the commanders of the accompanying ships to secure a rescue. The storm worsens by the minute; the commanders must return to their ships. After the sea has calmed down, the Pope summons the commanders a second time. Suddenly, the storm returns. The Pope stays at the ship's wheel and tries with all his might to steer it between the two columns, to which many anchors and countless hooks are fastened. The ships of the enemy start their attack again and want to sink the papal boat. Time and again, they try to throw explosives at the ship and fire all of their canons at it. Despite their passionate fight and the use of all weapons, the attack of the hostile ships fails, the sea is free and safe again, and the papal vessel continues on its way, despite considerable damage to both sides. Wind from the two columns repairs the damages and seals every leak. On the ships of the attackers, the gunpowder explodes, the rams break, and many vessels burst in two and sink into the sea. Suddenly, the Pope is struck by a bullet from the enemy. His helpers run towards him and try to help him, but later, another bullet hits him and he sinks to the floor lifeless. The enemy's fleet celebrates and screams. The commanders who are gathered on the papal ship re-elect a new Pope with such haste, that the announcement of the death of the old commander reaches the enemies at the same time as the message of his successor. The enemies lose all courage; the Papal ship, on the other hand, overcomes all obstacles and sails in between the two columns where it casts its anchor, and is fastened to them with strong chains. The foes flee, ramming and destroying each other. The small accompanying ships of the papal fleet row with full throttle back to the two columns and set their anchors as well. A great tranquility triumphs on the sea, a great tranquility triumphs."

At this point, Don Bosco asks Don Michele Rua, his successor, "What do you think of this story?" Don Michele answers, "It seems that the ship of the Pope is the Church, of which he is commander. The other ships are people, and the sea is the world. Those who defend the large ship are the devoted followers of the Pope; the others are his enemies, who seek to annihilate the Church at all costs. It seems to me that the two pillars are the veneration of Mary and the Holy Eucharist." Don Bosco replied, "Indeed, you have spoken well. Just one expression must be corrected: the ships of the enemy symbolize the persecution of the Church. They prepare the hardest toil for the Church. What has happened in the past is nothing in comparison to what is still to come. The ships symbolize the enemies of the Church, who try to sink the large vessel. Only two means exist to secure rescue from this confusion: the veneration of the Mother of God and frequent Communion." Jesus and Mary are the two pillars in the midst of the turbulent sea, who, if we unite ourselves to them through the strong chain of the Rosary, will save us from shipwreck.

On the day of his death, Don Bosco greeted Mary with the words: "Mother, tomorrow, tomorrow!" On January 31, 1888, he prayed the Angelus Prayer in the Church of Our Lady Help of Christians, during which this great devotee of Mary and Apostle of the Youth returned to his heavenly Teacher and Mother.

Prayer of St. Dominic Savio (Student of St. John Bosco)

O Mary, I give you my heart.
Grant me to be always yours.
Jesus and Mary,
be ever my friends;
and, for love of You,
grant that I might die a thousand deaths
rather than have the misfortune
of committing a single mortal sin.

FIFTH DAY

Mary—Mighty Advocate

Invocation of the Holy Spirit

Breathe in me, O Holy Spirit,
that my thoughts may all be holy.
Act in me, O Holy Spirit,
that my work, too, may be holy.
Draw my heart, O Holy Spirit,
that I love but what is holy.
Strengthen me, O Holy Spirit,
to defend all that is holy.
Guard me, then, O Holy Spirit,
that I always may be holy.
Amen.

(St. Augustine)

Scriptural Reading

The Wedding Feast at Cana

John 2: 1-9,11

On the third day there was a wedding at Cana in Galilee, and the mother of Jesus was there. Jesus also was invited to the wedding with his disciples. When the wine ran out, the mother of Jesus said to him, "They have no wine." And Jesus said to her, "Woman, what does this have to do with me? My hour has not yet come." His mother said to the servants, "Do whatever he tells you." Now there were six stone water jars there for the Jewish rites of purification, each holding twenty or thirty gallons. Jesus said to the servants, "Fill the jars with water." And they filled them up to the brim. And he said to them, "Now draw some out and take it to the master of the feast." So they took it. When the master of the feast tasted the water now become wine, (…). This, the first of his signs, Jesus did at Cana in Galilee, and manifested his glory. And his disciples believed in him.

Reflection

For thirty years, Jesus lived hidden in Nazareth; for thirty years, He was obedient to Mary and Joseph and lived the humble life of a carpenter. His public mission, his time of preaching and great miracles, was to number only three years. Would He not have to leave the home of His parents earlier, in order to give more glory to God, perform more miracles, and convert more people? Evidently not, since Jesus knew what He was doing. By His humility and His silent obedience He wanted to set an example for us. In this way, He glorified God more than through a life of great public interest.

His first miracle, the changing of water into wine, He performs out of obedience to His mother. When He calls her "woman," He does not intend to turn her away, but, as we will see in the use of this title on Golgotha, to honor her and give her prominence. His hour has not yet come, but Jesus does not want to refuse Mary's plea. Indeed, it seems as though He had shortened the time that was fixed from eternity, and revealed His glory through her intercession. For the sake of Mary, He begins His public works earlier and let that hour on

Golgotha draw closer, which, by calling her "woman," He references: the hour of our salvation! Mary's pleas move Heaven and Earth; they reach the heart of God, who always hears her! She indeed is the "almighty intercessor", since God cannot refuse her prayers: that is how much He loves and honors her! God gladly yields to her petitions because she never asks anything for herself or for something that could be displeasing to Him. She does not want anything else, only what God wants. That is the reason why she not only calls to the servants, but all of us Christians: "Do whatever He tells you!" It is a pleasure for God to fulfill her biddings. In hearing her intercession, He miraculously fulfills His holy will—namely, by the collaboration of His most lovely, humble, and noble creature!

We call upon Mary when we have run out of wine, that is, when we have a lack of strength to do good, or of true love and joy, because then we have only to offer our murky water, and she will ask her Son to change it into excellent wine. Yes, even before pronouncing our plea, she will intercede for us, since she knows our needs and wants to deliver us from the embarrassment of being helpless. This was what she did at the wedding feast at Cana, where she asked before the bridal party could. What a good Mother we have in Mary! With boundless trust we can approach her; with limitless love, we must thank her, since all the good that God has granted us, He grants through her hands. That is how he wants to honor His humble handmaid, who has always carried out His will.

Decade of the Rosary

The second Luminous Mystery: The transformation of water into wine at the Wedding Feast at Cana

We reflect how Jesus, the Divine Bridegroom of the Church, performed His first miracle, to proclaim the coming of the

Kingdom. He hears all the prayers of Mary, perfect image of
the Church, faithful Virgin, Mother of God's children.

Prayer to the Virgin Mary

O Holy Mary, my Mistress, into Your blessed trust and special
keeping, into the bosom of Your tender mercy, this day, every
day of my life and at the hour of my death, I commend my
soul and body; to You I entrust all my hopes and consolations,
all my trials and miseries, my life and the end of my life, that
through Your most holy intercession and Your merits, all my
actions may be ordered and disposed according to Your will
and that of Your Divine Son. Amen.

St. Aloysius Gonzaga

Closing Prayer

Lord, Holy Father, in Your wondrous will You have included
the Blessed Virgin Mary in the mysterious work of our
salvation. Grant that we listen to the Mother of Christ and do
what Your son taught us to do in the Gospel. He, who lives
and reigns with you in the Holy Spirit, one God forever and
ever. Amen

Spiritual Reading

The Example of Jesus for the consecration to Mary

When we meditate the incarnation of God we need to
wonder time and time again: God, who lives in the glory of
heavens, becomes man, yes, a small child, out of love for us.
Christ would have been able to come as radiant hero, maybe
accompanied by angels, into the world—strong, mighty, and

independent! No, he wanted to set an example of humility and love for us, and became subject to his mother, despite being her creator (cf. Lk 2:50) He chose and gave us Mary as the best, most beautiful, most secure and shortest way to our salvation. Like Jesus we want to wander on that path, to get to him safely and quickly!

From the *Treatise on True Devotion*

Our good Master stooped to enclose himself in the womb of the Blessed Virgin, a captive but loving slave, and to make himself subject to her for thirty years. As I said earlier, the human mind is bewildered when it reflects seriously upon this conduct of Incarnate Wisdom. He did not choose to give himself in a direct manner to the human race though he could easily have done so. He chose to come through the Virgin Mary. Thus he did not come into the world independently of others in the flower of his manhood, but he came as a frail little child dependent on the care and attention of his Mother. Consumed with the desire to give glory to God, his Father, and save the human race, he saw no better or shorter way to do so than by submitting completely to Mary. He did this not just for the first eight, ten or fifteen years of his life like other children, but for thirty years. He gave more glory to God, his Father, during all those years of submission and dependence than he would have given by spending them working miracles, preaching far and wide, and converting all mankind. Otherwise he would have done all these things. What immeasurable glory then do we give to God when, following the example of Jesus, we submit to Mary! With such a convincing and well- known example before us, can we be so foolish as to believe that there is a better and shorter way of giving God glory than by submitting ourselves to Mary, as Jesus did?[10]

---

10. *True Devotion* V, 139.

From the Lives of the Saints

St. Aloysius of Gonzaga

Seldom is a saint as distorted in pious art as St. Aloysius of
Gonzaga has been. An unworldly boy hovering over colorful
clouds, as a childish youngster with transfigured facial features,
a sweet smile and eyes lifted up to heaven. He was depicted
much like a fantasy figure from a fairy tale, who had never even
imagined the temptations, sufferings, difficulties, and problems
of this world, which are part of most people's daily lives. The
truth is that Aloysius was a very different kind of man, who
realized the meaning of life at a very early age and knew that
material riches, a career, and sensual pleasures—which would
have been possible due to his noble background—could not
make him happy. That is the reason why he decisively took a
step away from his inheritance, which would have given him
a life with no worries or sufferings, and entered the order of
the Jesuits with determination to preach the Gospel in the
streets, in the squares, in schools, and in hospitals. Aloysius
did not hover over silky clouds, but wanted to go to the roads
to care for the most needy and sick. The seemingly delicate
and weak boy, the unworldly saint, who on many prayer cards
is depicted with a white surplice and a faint lily, was a young
man who possessed heroic courage, carried the sick to the
hospital on his shoulders, and, not only washed and dressed
their wounds, but also cared for their souls. Aloysius knew life
with its highs and lows, its temptations and dangers. With the
full passion of a saint, he battled against sin and risked the
adventure of the faith.

Aloysius was the son of a powerful prince. Riches and
worldly happiness lay at his feet. But full of disgust, he turned
away from the vain games of the noble court, repulsed by the
blind yearning for power and sensual pleasure. When Ferdi-

nand Gonzaga brought his two sons, Aloysius and Rudolf, to Florence in order to entrust them to the lush atmosphere of the Medicis, Aloysius came from the protected and quiet Castiglione to the colorful life of the court where races, parties, dances, and public entertainment occupied the days. From the quiet of the countryside and his family he came into the center of political power and experienced the egotistical strive for career and personal prestige, which took hold even of those who were educated at court.

The eight-year-old boy was immediately faced with the decision to do the same or to refuse participating from the beginning. Despite his youth, Aloysius had the courage to say "no," without retreating into solitude or becoming bitter. With excitement and curiosity, he observed the novelties of the large city, but was preparing a part of his heart to be solely dedicated to Jesus and Mary. Even while playing with children his own age, and taking an active part in the spectacles of the court, even in the loudest confusion, he lived in the knowledge that Jesus and Mary were close.

Before an image of Our Lady, he devoted himself to the Mother of God and pleaded to Mary for one grace in particular: to protect him against all temptations of purity. Aloysius listened to the inappropriate jokes of his companions day in and day out. He witnessed all kinds of flirtations and romances at court, and it was all too clear that this heated sensual atmosphere would suffocate every true happiness and innocence. The first great step towards sanctity was one that Aloysius had already found as a child: only that which does not transgress the commandments of God can make one happy. Therefore he did not want his heart distracted by the fascinating appeal of the sensual, the misconceptions of human love and passion, by apathetic satisfaction and dishonest advances.

The courtly life could not fulfill Aloysius, and he recognized how vain, superficial and fleeing were the entertainments of many nobles. He was shocked by the compromises, intrigues and mean plans men were willing to make, in order to have a short lasting material advantage or to step up in the hierarchy. "What does that mean for me in eternity?" he asked repeatedly. He wanted to be happy much more than his friends did, who gave up real happiness for the appearances of a rich man's life. Aloysius wanted more—"magis," as St. Ignatius calls it—than the life of the nobles could give him. From Florence, the two brothers went to the court of the Duke of Mantua. Already in Florence the young prince was suffering from a stomach condition. In Mantua he began to complain of a problem with his gall bladder, which he strongly fought with hunger. His mother was shocked when he returned pale and really lean. Since he returned to better health, she calmed down but observed attentively the changes that he underwent during those maturing years. Through the Catechism of St. Peter Canisius, Aloysius learned what meditation was. He experienced the kind of inner joy that is triggered by prayer, and just as St. Teresa of Avila, he felt as if he were resting with a friend. Was there anything more that the Duke of Mantua could offer him? Again and again Aloysius wanted to retreat into a corner of the palace to think about religious truths and seek closeness with Jesus and Mary.

His inclination was aided by St. Charles Borromeo, who gave him his first Holy Communion. From that day on his thoughts circled around this wondrous mystery, so much so that common entertainment appeared to him shallow and void in comparison to the Eucharist. What is the largest gold treasure of a king in comparison to God Himself, who awaits us in the Tabernacle, because He loves us? Already at that time it was clear to him, that he could never lead the life of a prince, but the uncertainty of his future way weighted heavily on him. He chastised himself with many acts of penance, struggled for clarity with prayer, and fought with his father because of his refusal to join the theater and parties at court.

The Margrave had all of his hopes on Aloysius, who was his eldest son.[11] Aloysius seems to be the born statesman: intelligent with a self-confident presence. While the whole Gonzaga family enjoyed the following years in Madrid in the grace of the king of Spain, Aloysius was accepted by him as a page. During that time, the Margrave tried to expel the seemingly ridiculous ideas from his head. He accomplished the very opposite. Even the glamour of the proud court did not convince the boy to turn away from his serious philosophical and mathematical studies. His spiritual director was the rector of the Jesuit College in Madrid. Aloysius preferred to kneel in prayer at the Jesuit Church, and it was there, on the Feast of the Assumption of Mary in the year 1583, that he followed the call to enter the Society of Jesus. As soon as he announced the idea to his family, his father threatened him with lashing. Two years passed during which Ferdinand Gonzaga tried everything he could to lead Aloysius away from his path. His efforts were in vain! The boy held fast to his vocation and his passionate zeal in prayer. His desire to make his love for Christ visible through acts of penance seemed to grow with the opposition of his father. One day, the Margrave saw how his son had chastised himself while praying the penitential Psalm, "Miserere": "Behold, I was shaped in wickedness: and in sin did my mother conceive me." The Margrave was stunned and gave him permission to leave. A certificate of abdication in favor of his younger brother was signed and validated by the king. In October 1585, he traveled to the Roman novitiate of the Jesuits.

---

11. Margrave was originally the medieval title for the military commander assigned to maintain the defense of one of the border provinces of the Holy Roman Empire or of a kingdom.

The prince had become a poor religious. In the novitiate, he began his theological studies, and was almost constantly beset by headaches and insomnia. Only through conscientiousness and loyalty to his duty did he continue in his studies. He zealously strove for a deeper relationship with God, whom he sought in meditative prayer and in pious reception of the Sacraments.

Then, in 1591, the Black Death approached. Immediately, Aloysius asked for permission to care for the victims of the plague. After long reluctance, his wish was granted. Despite the natural revulsion, he cared for even the most ghastly cases, until he himself was stricken with the plague on March 3, 1591. His body fought for three months against the lurking poison in his veins. He foresaw the day and hour of his death. On June 21, at the age of twenty-three he was called to the judgment throne of Jesus Christ, where he could receive an answer to the question: "What value does this have for eternity?"

Aloysius died as a young man who was passionately in love with Christ, whose friendship he sought to win anew every day in silent meditation and interior prayer before the Tabernacle, in the childlike veneration of His Holy Mother and in selflessly caring for the sick and the dying. Everything that Aloysius had accomplished in his short life, he chose to do with youthful vigor. Therefore, the Church raised him to be the patron of youth, the heavenly friend who wishes to help people in midst of the wearying allures of this world, to find and chose the steep path which alone leads to true happiness.

Prayer to the Mother of God

We believe, O Mother, in your great might,
Though you be hidden as a darkest night.
We believe in your victorious strength
Though our desires may find no recompense.

We love you, Mother, who so tenderly
Love each and all of us unceasingly.
We love you, too, when you do not bestow
You endless riches on us here below.
Yet in your mercy and benevolence
Increase our faith and childlike confidence.

O let us always see your loving care
That, strong in faith, we do not fear to dare
But face the future sure of victory,
Looking to you for guidance trustfully.
Our love will free us from all earthly ties
That, eager and prepared for sacrifice,
We offer life and love and loyalty
Serving you now and in eternity.
Amen.

Schoenstatt prayer, "Childlike Trust"

SIXTH DAY

Mary—Mother of Sorrows

Invocation of the Holy Spirit

Breathe in me, O Holy Spirit,
that my thoughts may all be holy.
Act in me, O Holy Spirit,
that my work, too, may be holy.
Draw my heart, O Holy Spirit,
that I love but what is holy.
Strengthen me, O Holy Spirit,
to defend all that is holy.
Guard me, then, O Holy Spirit,
that I always may be holy.
Amen.

(St. Augustine)

Scripture Reading

Mark 15: 16-22

"And the soldiers led him away inside the palace, and they called together the whole battalion. And they clothed him in a purple cloak, and twisting together a crown of thorns, they put it on him. And they began to salute him, "Hail, King of the Jews!" And they were striking his head with a reed and spitting on him and kneeling down in homage to him. And when they had mocked him, they stripped him of the purple cloak and put his own clothes on him. And they led him out to crucify him.

And they compelled a passerby, Simon of Cyrene, who was coming in from the country, the father of Alexander and Rufus, to carry his cross. And they brought him to the place called Golgotha (which means Place of a Skull)."

Reflection

During the public life of Jesus, Mary remains almost always in the background. When the time of His suffering draws near, she insists on remaining by His side. Amidst the mass of people, the Mother of Jesus experiences the sentencing of her innocent Son, and watches as He is crowned with thorns, dripping with blood in front of the Praetorium. She hears the spiteful screams: "Crucify Him!" What sufferings she must undergo, how deeply her heart is wounded by the hatred of these people! But Mary is not filled with outrage; she knows that Jesus is the Servant of the Lord, prophesied by Isaiah, who will suffer and die on behalf of many. She remains strong even in these hours of pain. What a brave woman, what a wonderful mother!

On the Way of the Passion, Mother and Son meet. What grief for Jesus to see His own mother in such anguish! What a comfort it was for Him to know that He had a companion by His side; she was the only one, as she was without sin, who had no fault in His suffering. Their eyes meet, full of grief and sorrow! And even though the Savior tries to find words to comfort the crying women, he is quiet before Mary. He knows that she is strong enough to go all the way with Him. Thankful, He acknowledges the closeness of Mary His Mother, who helps him more in His carrying the Cross to Golgotha than Simon ever could, and who gives Him more comfort than Veronica did through her last act of love.

Even though Mary knows that it is our sins that have burdened her Son with the Cross, she is full of love for us, and wants to help us when pain and distress burden us. She is the good Mother who stands by the wayside in our lives, who helps us by making everything easier. She shows us her love and devotion even more when we suffer, because we unite ourselves with her Son in those moments. With the same tenderness and care that she had in Jerusalem, she will stand by our side when we have to carry our Cross to Golgotha. She helps us in our daily efforts to accept our sufferings and to follow Jesus. When it seems to be too difficult and painful, then we can gaze upon our lovely Mother. Like a good mother at the bedside of her sick child, she will whisper to us in our grimmest hours: "Do not be afraid, I am here!"

Decade of the Rosary

The fourth Sorrowful Mystery: The Carrying of the Cross
Let us ask pardon of Jesus and Mary, because our sins have made His Cross so heavy.

Prayer to the Mother of God

Litany of Loreto

Lord, have mercy.	*Lord, have mercy.*
Christ, have mercy.	*Christ, have mercy.*
Lord, have mercy.	*Lord, have mercy.*
Christ, hear us.	*Christ, graciously hear us.*
God, the Father of heaven,	*Have mercy on us.*

God the Son, Redeemer of the world, *Have mercy on us.*
God the Holy Spirit,   *Have mercy on us.*
Holy Trinity, one God,   *Have mercy on us.*

Response for the following invocations: *Pray for us.*

Holy Mary
Holy Mother of God
Holy Virgin of virgin,
Mother of Christ
Mother of the Church
Mother of divine grace
Mother most pure
Mother most chaste
Mother inviolate
Mother undefiled
Mother most amiable
Mother most admirable
Mother of good counsel
Mother of our Creator
Mother of our Savior
Virgin most prudent
Virgin most venerable
Virgin most renowned
Virgin most powerful
Virgin most merciful
Virgin most faithful
Mirror of justice
Seat of wisdom

Cause of our joy

Spiritual vessel

Vessel of honor

Singular vessel of devotion

Mystical rose

Tower of David

Tower of ivory

House of gold,

Ark of the covenant

Gate of heaven

Morning star

Health of the sick

Refuge of sinners

Comforter of the afflicted

Help of Christians

Queen of angels

Queen of patriarchs

Queen of prophets

Queen of apostles

Queen of martyrs

Queen of confessors

Queen of virgins

Queen of all saints

Queen conceived without original sin

Queen assumed into heaven

Queen of the most holy Rosary

Queen of families

Queen of peace

Lamb of God, You take away the sins of the world;
Spare us, O Lord.
Lamb of God, You take away the sins of the world;
Graciously hear us, O Lord.
Lamb of God, Your take away the sins of the world;
Have mercy on us.

V. Pray for us, O Holy Mother of God.
R. *That we may be made worthy of the promises of Christ.*

Closing Prayer

Lord, our God, in accordance with Your will, Mary accompanied her Son on His Way of the Cross as a sorrowful Mother. Help us to follow His path and keep us on the way, which alone leads to salvation. This we ask through Jesus Christ, our Lord and God, who reigns with You in the Holy Spirit, one Lord forever and ever. Amen.

Spiritual Reading

The Virgin Mary makes our good works pleasing to her Son

Jesus Christ, the incarnate son of God is and will remain forever the son of Mary. We call him Lord and God, Mary can say to him: My son! How can he, who on earth obeyed the 4th Commandment with intensive care, how can he refuse a wish from his mother? What we give to Mary, Jesus will accept with love. If we consecrate ourselves to Mary completely, God will embrace us mercifully.

From the *Treatise on True Devotion*

Since by this devotion we give to our Lord, through the hands of his holy Mother, all our good works, she purifies them, making them beautiful and acceptable to her Son.

1. Mary purifies them of every taint of self-love

Her hands have never been known to be idle or uncreative. They purify everything they touch. As soon as the Blessed Virgin receives our good works, she removes any blemish or imperfection she may find in them.

2. She enriches our good works by adorning them with her own merits and virtues.

It is as if a poor peasant, wishing to win the friendship and favor of the king, were to go the queen and give her an apple—his only possession—for her to offer it to the king. The queen, accepting the peasant's humble gift, puts it on a beautiful golden dish and presents it to the king on behalf of the peasant. The apple in itself would not be a gift worthy of a king, but presented by the queen in person on a dish of gold, it becomes fit for any king.

3. Mary presents our good works to Jesus.

She does not keep anything we offer for herself, as if she were our last end, but unfailingly gives everything to Jesus. So by the very fact we give anything to her, we are giving it to Jesus. Whenever we praise and glorify her, she sings today as she did on the day Elizabeth praised her, "My soul glorifies the Lord."

4. At Mary's request, Jesus accepts the gift of our good works

But when we present something to him by the pure, virginal hands of his beloved Mother, we take him by his weak side, in a manner of speaking. He does not consider so much the present itself as the person who offers it. Thus Mary, who is never slighted by her Son but is always well received, prevails upon him to accept with pleasure everything she offers him,

regardless of its value. Mary has only to present the gift for
Jesus graciously to accept it. This is what St. Bernard strongly
recommended to all those he was guiding along the pathway
to perfection. "When you want to offer something to God, to
be welcomed by him, be sure to offer it through the worthy
Mother of God, if you do not wish to see it rejected."[12]

From the Lives of the Saints

Saint Thérèse of the Child Jesus (Thérèse of Lisieux)

Saint Thérèse of Lisieux, born in Alençon, France on January
2, 1873, is often referred to as "the little one." Her short life of
twenty four years, which began hidden in her parents' home
and ended in the Carmel of Lisieux, cannot be compared to
that of St. Teresa of Avila, the "great" Spanish reformer of
the Order of the Carmelites who was restless in founding new
monasteries and writing spiritual texts. But Thérèse's name
does belong alongside St. Catherine of Siena, to the group
of four women upon whom the honorary title of "Doctor
of the Church" has been bestowed. In her yearning to love
God and with her never-ending zeal to live her life completely
for Christ and His Church, the Saint from Lisieux is no less
important than her great spiritual Mother of Avila. She writes
in her world-famous biography, "Story of a Soul," about the
burning desire she had as a child to become a Saint: "I also
understood that there are many degrees of holiness, that each
soul is free to respond to the call of Our Lord, to do much
or little for His Love— to choose among the sacrifices He
asks. And then also, as in the days of my childhood, I cried
out: "My God, I choose everything, I will not be a Saint only
partially, I am not afraid to suffer for You, I only fear one

---

12. *True Devotion*, 146–149.

thing, and that is to do my own will. Accept the offering of my will, for I choose all that You willest!"

Thérèse of Lisieux became a colossal Saint, not through noticeable acts or glorious works, but by the silent fulfillment of her duty to love, which was later described as the "little way" of holiness. In this way, she consequently followed Mary, according to the example and hand-in-hand with the one who leads everyone to Jesus, to whom she fully entrusted herself. A powerful experience in her devotion to the Mother of God was when she was miraculously healed as a ten-year-old girl since doctors were unable to help her. Thérèse witnessed the miracle. The whole family had prayed a novena to the Blessed Virgin Mary for her. Then one day Thérèse saw how the statue of Mary in her room started to move: "Suddenly the statue came to life! The dear Mother of God became all beautiful, so beautiful that I will never find an expression to describe this divine kind of beauty! Her face radiated an unspeakable meek kindness and tenderness. What touched me in the depth of my soul was her enchanting smile." From this moment on, Thérèse was healed. Her sickness vanished, but the gentle smile of the Mother of God remained imprinted on her soul. It would accompany her for the rest of her life and give her the strength to live for Jesus Christ, to suffer for Him and to love Him—to whom she would be espoused in the Carmel, above all things.

It is this insatiable passion for Christ that marked and guided the whole life of Thérèse. From her childhood, the desire grew within her to follow the older sisters into the monastery in order to belong fully to Jesus. Her request to enter was refused due to her young age, and the local bishop was unwilling to help her. She went on a pilgrimage to Rome, and during one of the general audiences, she approached Pope Leo XIII (on November 20, 1887) with her plea to enter the Carmel at the young age of fifteen. The Pope's response did not satisfy her at first: "My child, do what your superiors tell you!"—"But Holy Father, if you said yes, then all would agree!" Thérèse's stubbornness, which went against the protocol of the Papal court—since it was expressly forbidden for pilgrims to speak to the Pope directly—seemed to have been a success, as Leo XIII answered her, "Well then, well then... you will enter, if the good God wills it!"

Soon after her trip to Rome all of her difficulties vanished. She entered the Carmel of Lisieux on April 9, 1888, on the feast of the Annunciation, which was moved to a different date that year since it coincided with Lent. On the liturgical feast of that day, the "fiat" of the Virgin of Nazareth, which brought the Savior of all mankind into the world, became the center of attention equally for Thérèse. The words: "Let it be done to me according to Your word" marked Thérèse's will to emulate the humility of Mary. Just as Mary, she understood her "yes" to the will of God as being a co-worker in salvation. To the question of why she chose the Carmel, Thérèse answered, "I came here to save souls and to pray especially for priests."

Characteristic of Thérèse's spirituality was her childlike trust, expecting and hoping for everything from God. Audacity, spontaneity, and sometimes even mischievous formulations characterized her devotion to Mary. For example, St. Thérèse's prayer, "O Mary, if I were the queen of heaven and you were Thérèse, I would prefer to be Thérèse, so that you could become the queen of heaven!" On another occasion, she cried out in wonder after having gazed upon a statue of Mary, "Who could have created the Holy Mother of God?"

The religious life of St. Thérèse lasted only a short while and lacked every spectacular event. Faithful and hidden, she walked her "little way" day by day at Mary's side and always with her gaze fixed on Jesus, her beloved Spouse. The passionate longing always remains alive in her heart to become a great saint, who would surpass all saints in heaven with her love and her great acts for the Church. She wished to do everything imaginable for Christ: "I feel the vocation of the warrior, the priest, the apostle, the doctor, the martyr. Finally, I feel the need and the desire of carrying out the most heroic deeds for You, O Jesus. I feel within me the vocation of the priest. With what love, O Jesus, would I take You in my hands when, at my voice, You would come down from heaven. And with what love would I give You to souls! But alas! Ah! In spite of my littleness, I would like to enlighten souls as did the Prophets and the Doctors. I have the vocation of the Apostle. I would like to travel over the whole earth to preach Your Name and to plant Your glorious Cross in the soil of nonbelievers. But O, my Beloved, one mission alone would not be sufficient for me, I would want to preach the Gospel on all the five continents simultaneously and even to the most remote isles."

Even more passionately, more longingly, more "foolishly," does Thérèse unceasingly speak of her desire to become a martyr: "Martyrdom was the dream of my youth and this dream has grown within me in Carmel's cloisters. But here again, I feel that my dream is a folly, for I cannot confine myself to desiring one kind of martyrdom. To satisfy me I need all. Like You, my Adorable Spouse, I would be scourged and crucified. I would die flayed like St. Bartholomew. I would be plunged into boiling oil like St. John; I would undergo all the tortures inflicted upon the martyrs. I would be crushed by the teeth of the raging lions like St. Ignatius of Antioch to become bread that is worthy of God." Thérèse does not quarrel with her religious vocation; she does not rebel against the priesthood, which is exclusively for men, nor does she plunge herself into crazy dreams to escape daily reality. No, she keeps a true Christian longing for holiness alive within herself. The little nun who never left the Carmel has become a Doctor of the Church and a second Patroness of world missions. In her boundless trust, and prayer embracing all nations, she overcame the walls of her convent and conquered the whole world for the kingdom of Christ. Yes, especially in the small, enclosed cell in Carmel she found her own proper vocation, which embraced all others of whom she dreamed: "I understood that if the Church had a body composed of different members, the most necessary and most noble of all could not be lacking to it, and so I understood that the Church had a heart and that this heart was burning with love. I understood that it was love alone that made the Church's members act, that if love were ever extinguished, apostles would not proclaim the Gospel and martyrs would refuse to shed their blood. I understood that love includes all vocations... Then in the excess of my delirious joy, I cried out: 'O Jesus, my Love... at last I have found my vocation; my vocation is Love!'"

Foremost in the last moments of her life, Thérèse gave witness to this love when she not only suffered physically, but also spiritually, as a darkness of soul pushed her to the limits of her powers. Her once radiant faith is plunged into darkness and strong doubts haunt her, so that she no longer feels any kind of security in her soul and remains tied to God only by her will. She copies the Creed with the determination to carry it with her at all times, as a precious witness to truth, her mouth utters prayers when they are apparently reduced to just words and when her heart seems as cold as ice. In these last months, she writes, "I cannot pray. I can only look at Mary and say, 'Jesus'!"

The young "little" saintly Thérèse died of tuberculosis at only twenty-four years of age. She had chosen the name "of the Child of Jesus" for her daily spirituality. In her final dark hours, it was again Mary in whose smile Thérèse took refuge in order to find strength and comfort. In her cell, a statue of the Mother of God was propped up, the same miraculous statue from her childhood. Ceaselessly, Thérèse looks at her:

"Never before did she seem so beautiful... but today it is the statue. As you know, in the past it was not the statue. O, how much I love the Virgin Mary! If I had been a priest, how beautifully would I have spoken about her. She is always said to be unapproachable, but we should show how we can indeed emulate her. She is more a mother than a queen!"

On September 30, 1897, the day of her death, she told the nurse: "I have ardently prayed to Mary. But it is pure agony without comfort: Mary, hasten to my aid! O, you know that I am suffocating!" But now the hour of fulfilling Thérèse's longing had come, which she explained in her autobiography as the comparison between a weak bird and a soaring eagle: "How can an imperfect soul, like mine, yearn for the fullness of love? But how could my trust have boundaries? The day will come—that is what I trust—when you will melt me together with you and carry me up to the epicenter of love." Thérèse's childlike audacity and her seemingly unending trust in God brought light in the last darkness. Love is all that will be left and all that will reach into the next life: "I have never done anything other than love God; He will repay me with His love. Yes, I will live in paradise by doing good on earth." According to this promise, St. Thérèse is often shown with rose petals that she throws from her hands—a symbol of the graces she ask for the Church on earth, because in heaven also, the little Thérèse desires to communicate the love of God to all men.

Prayer of St. Thérèse of Lisieux to the Mother of God

You make me feel that it is not impossible to follow in your footsteps, O Queen of the elect. You made visible the narrow road to Heaven while always practicing the humblest virtues. Near you, Mary, I like to remain little.

Mary—Our Mother

Invocation of the Holy Spirit

Breathe in me, O Holy Spirit,
that my thoughts may all be holy.
Act in me, O Holy Spirit,
that my work, too, may be holy.
Draw my heart, O Holy Spirit,
that I love but what is holy.
Strengthen me, O Holy Spirit,
to defend all that is holy.
Guard me, then, O Holy Spirit,
that I always may be holy.
Amen.

(St. Augustine)

Scripture Reading

Mary at the foot of the Cross

John 19: 25-27

But standing beside the Cross of Jesus were His mother, His
mother's sister, Mary, the wife of Clopas, and Mary Magdalene.
When Jesus saw His mother and the disciple whom He loved

standing nearby, He said to His mother, "Woman, behold, your son!" Then He said to the disciple, "Behold, your mother!" And from that hour the disciple took her to his own home.

7.3 *Reflection*

The Mother of Christ follows the Way of the Cross until the very end. All of the Apostles, except St. John, had fled; Mary, on the other hand, courageously remains at the foot of the Cross. She experiences Jesus being nailed to the wood. Every hit of the hammer wounds her own heart; she suffers as only a mourning mother could suffer. What a tremendous pain! Now the hour has come, which Simeon had prophesied in the Temple: "Your heart will be pierced by a sword!" But the hour of redemption has also come, because by His death on the wood of the Cross, Christ conquers the old serpent that had brought sin and death into the world on the tree in Paradise. Mary is the new Eve, who suffers with Christ in order to bring the whole world to salvation. "Mary is the model of union with Christ. The life of the Holy Virgin was the life of a woman of her people: Mary prayed, she worked, she went to the synagogue… But every action was carried out in perfect union with Jesus. This union finds its culmination on Calvary: here Mary is united to the Son in the martyrdom of her heart and in the offering of his life to the Father for the salvation of humanity. Our Lady shared in the pain of the Son and accepted with him the will of the Father, in that obedience that bears fruit, that grants the true victory over evil and death. The reality Mary teaches us is very beautiful: to always be united with Jesus. We can ask ourselves: do we remember Jesus only when something goes wrong and we are in need, or is ours a constant relation, a deep friendship, even when it means following him on the way of the Cross? Let us ask the Lord to grant us his grace, his strength, so that the model of Mary, Mother of the Church, may be reflected in our lives and in the life of every ecclesial community. So be it!"[13] Now the prophecy is fulfilled, which God gave to our forefathers: "I will put enmity between you and the woman, and between your offspring and her offspring; she shall bruise your head, and you shall bruise his heel!" (Cf. Gen 3:15).

Christ knows that these ancient words are coming true. That is why He calls His mother, "woman," because as Eve became the mother of all men, Christ makes Mary the Mother of all the redeemed in the hour of His death. He not only sacrifices His life for us, but He gives us the most precious and beautiful good that He had on earth: His own Mother. Mary knows the meaning of this hour. She embraces John and all people as her children. From then on, all of her love has been granted to those for whom her Son poured out His blood. His last testament is sacred to her.

We can imagine how thankful St. John was, that Jesus had given him Mary as a Mother. We also know from Sacred Scripture, that he took her into his home and cared for her. Let us, too, take on Mary as our Mother. She is the great inheritance that Jesus has given us. She wants to be our Mother, if we would only accept her, if we would give ourselves to her completely. She is indeed our Mother already, because we owe our lives to her, since she has given us Christ and has given us salvation on Calvary with Him.

Decade of the Rosary

The fifth Sorrowful Mystery: Jesus is crucified and dies on the Cross for us
We desire to stand under the Cross with Mary and trustingly grasp her hand, so that she can become our Mother.

---

13. Pope Francis, *Discourse at General Audience* (October 23, 2013).

Prayer to Mary (Stabat Mater)

At the cross her station keeping,
Mary stood in sorrow weeping
When her Son was crucified.

While she waited in her anguish,
Seeing Christ in torment languish,
Bitter sorrow pierced her heart.

With what pain and desolation,
With what noble resignation,
Mary watched her dying Son.

Ever-patient in her yearning
Though her tear-filled eyes were burning,
Mary gazed upon her Son.

Who, that sorrow contemplating,
On that passion meditating,
Would not share the Virgin's grief?

Christ she saw, for our salvation,
Scourged with cruel acclamation,
Bruised and beaten by the rod.

Christ she saw with life-blood failing,
All her anguish unavailing,
Saw him breathe his very last.

Mary, fount of love's devotion,
Let me share with true emotion
All the sorrow you endured.

Virgin, ever interceding,
Hear me in my fervent pleading:
Fire me with your love of Christ.

Mother, may this prayer be granted:
That Christ's love may be implanted
In the depths of my poor soul.

At the cross, your sorrow sharing,
All your grief and torment bearing,
Let me stand and mourn with you.

Fairest maid of all creation,
Queen of hope and consolation,
Let me feel your grief sublime.

Virgin, in your love befriend me,
At the Judgment Day defend me.
Help me by your constant prayer.

Savior, when my life shall leave me,
Through your mother's prayers receive me
With the fruits of victory.

Virgin of all virgins blest!
Listen to my fond request:
Let me share your grief divine

Let me, to my latest breath,
In my body bear the death
Of your dying Son divine.

Wounded with His every wound,
Steep my soul till it has swooned
In His very Blood away.

Be to me, O Virgin, nigh,
Lest in flames I burn and die,
In His awe-full judgment day.

Savior, when my life shall leave me,
Through your mother's prayers receive me
With the fruits of victory.

While my body here decays
May my soul your goodness praise,
Safe in heaven eternally. Amen Alleluia.

Closing Prayer

Merciful God, through the Precious Blood of Your Son, You
have reconciled the world to Yourself and at the foot of the
Cross have entrusted His Mother to be our Mother also. By
the intercession of the Blessed Virgin Mary forgive our sins.
this we ask through Our Lord Jesus Christ, Your Son, who
lives and reigns with You in the unity of the Holy Spirit, one
God for ever and ever. Amen.

Spiritual Readings

Entrust everything to Mary

Everything that we give to Mary, she will look after with great
care. If we consecrate ourselves to her, she will guard and
protect us as her very own and keep us as the apple of her eye.
Everything, all the prayers and works we offer to her Immaculate

heart, she will enrich and pay interest for. Yes, we can compare the pure heart of Mary, which is full of grace, with a bank account into which we put our pennies. Our heavenly mother is able to draw capital from it and to expand our treasure in heaven. With her, all our internal and external riches are kept safe, so that no thief can steal them (cf. Lk 12:33).

From the *Treatise on True Devotion*

Moved by pure love, this good Mother always accepts whatever is given her in trust, and, once she accepts something, she finds herself in justice by a contract of trusteeship to keep it safe. Is not someone to whom I entrust the sum of a thousand francs obliged to keep it safe for me so that if it were lost through his negligence he would be responsible for it in strict justice? But nothing we entrust to the faithful Virgin will ever be lost through her negligence. Heaven and earth would pass away sooner than Mary would neglect or betray those who trusted in her.

Do not leave your gold and silver in your own safes, which have already been broken into and rifled many times by the evil one. They are too small, too flimsy and too old to contain such great and priceless possessions. Do not put pure and clear water from the spring into vessels fouled and infected by sin. Even if sin is no longer there, its odor persists and the water would be contaminated. You do not put choice wine into old casks that have contained sour wine. You would spoil the good wine and run the risk of losing it.

Pour into the bosom and heart of Mary all your precious possessions, all your graces and virtues. She is a spiritual vessel, a vessel of honor, a singular vessel of devotion. Ever since God personally hid himself with all his perfections in this vessel, it has become completely spiritual, and the spiritual abode of all spiritual souls. It has become honorable and has been the throne of honor for the greatest saints in heaven. It has become outstanding in devotion and the home of those renowned for gentleness, grace and virtue. Moreover, it has become as rich as a house of gold, as strong as a tower of David and as pure as a tower of ivory.

Nevertheless, after this digression, I say to both the critics and the devout that the Blessed Virgin, the most reliable and generous of all God's creatures, never lets herself be surpassed by anyone in love and generosity. For the little that is given to her, she gives generously of what she has received from God. Consequently, if a person gives himself to her without reserve, she gives herself also without reserve to that person provided his confidence in her is not presumptuous and he does his best to practice virtue and curb his passions.[14]

From the Lives of the Saints

St. Maria Goretti

Every year many people are victims of crimes, and the news about sexually abused children, or the brutal rapes of defenseless victims, always shocks us. Why is it that we remember this twelve year-old girl who was murdered in 1902? Maria Goretti died defending her dignity as a woman, after refusing to submit when a man desired to use her as a mere object of satisfaction. She wanted to remain pure—a concept that today often seems old-fashioned and prudish—but which Christ Himself included in the beatitudes, praising those with a sincere, radiant, and innocent heart. This purity, which signifies both the avoidance of sin in general and the struggle for chastity, is also attainable in our era. The life of Maria Goretti and her heroic decision proves that. Her death was not just a tragic accident. No, Maria Goretti died with a clear and complete understanding of her ideal.

---

14. *True Devotion*, 176–181.

Maria's mother suffered the hard yoke of bitter poverty. Even more, Marietta, who was born in 1890, had to let go of her beloved "babbo" (daddy), who died very early of malaria. She never passed by the wall of the cemetery without saying a short prayer for the repose of his soul. On his lap she learned to say the names of Jesus and Mary, and it was he who taught her the sign of the Cross and told her about the life of the Holy Family. Her parents could not afford to send her to school. She offered up her first Communion for her "babbo" (daddy), which she received at the age of eleven in the parish church of Nettuno. The brown-haired girl with dark eyes wandered often along the sunny, eleven-kilometer road to Nettuno. Maria Goretti yearned for Jesus, her only friend, to whom she could be so close during Holy Mass and in Holy Communion.

Like a mother, Maria cared for her siblings for whom she had taken responsibility for at an early age. When they were still hungry after a meal, she secretly gave them her own food. Maria was quiet when her mother Assunta screamed at her after an oversight. Obediently and modestly, she worked at patching her used clothes, which were a gift from her neighbor. The family could not afford a new skirt or a fashionable blouse.

The day's work ended by praying the daily Rosary together. It was led, of course, by Maria. The rosary was one of her favorite prayers, since with Mary she found comfort in Jesus for this hard and poor life which denied her a carefree and happy childhood. At least for a short time, the prayer gave her tranquility during the long workday; it let her breathe and find strength. She prayed a second Rosary almost every night in bed until she fell asleep completely exhausted.

Into this poor, dutiful life a tempter appeared, Alessandro Serenelli. The nineteen-year-old boy lived with his violent, alcoholic father next door to the Gorettis.

Maria once complained to her mother about the suggestive talk and ambiguous jokes that the girls made when they drew water from the well, but unfortunately, she kept quiet about how Alessandro had stalked her twice in the course of the month. Only on her deathbed did she speak about it reluctantly. She apologized for not having said anything due to her embarrassment.

In the eyes of Alessandro, Maria Goretti was nothing more than one of those girls who decorated the walls of his room—a carnal object of his desire, a target of his passion. Immodesty can draw the soul to mundane things in such a way that it becomes dark and blind to almost everything that is good and beautiful. The dignity of the other person, their life and happiness, their love and friendship count for nothing; their sexuality is reduced to the merely material realm. One's neighbor becomes a material object, and his or her body, a means to selfish gratification.

Maria, who suffered greatly from the wooing of Alessandro, became more and more depressed. She did everything to avoid the boy, which was not easy, since she needed to care for the household and laundry of the two Serenellis as well.

The fateful day was July 5, 1902. Only a few weeks before, Maria had heard a homily about the Passion of Christ in Conca. She was deeply moved and wanted to keep the resolution she had made: "It is better to die than to sin!" While her Mother Assunta and the neighbors were threshing with the oxen, Alessandro took advantage of the opportunity. However, Maria seemed to have had a premonition. She sat down at the front porch doing her patchwork and laid her youngest sister, who was asleep, beside her for greater protection. The boy dragged her forcefully into the house. She warned him in vain that he would go to hell if he willfully insisted. Alessandro, blinded by passion, threatened her with death, and Maria still strongly resisted against this horrible attempt to abuse her. She did not want to consent to a deed which she knew to be a sin for Alessandro—not even at the cost of her life. The boy stabbed her fourteen times before she fell to the floor. Her screams were not heard amidst the noise of the threshing.

On that very morning, she spontaneously said that she would like to receive Communion. Now she would receive her Savior before her death in the hospital of Nettuno. At that time, she said to her parish priest, Don Signori, "Yes, I forgive Alessandro, for the love of Jesus, and I want him to come to heaven with me." The doctors operated for two hours without anesthesia, but were unable to save her life. In excruciating pain, Maria called for her "babbo." She accepted, for the love of God the directives of the doctors, who had forbidden her mother from being next to her daughter on her final night.

On her deathbed, she was so full of joy that she could still consecrate herself to the Mother of God in the words: "The Mother of God awaits me." She died on Sunday, July 6. Adorned with a blue ribbon as a child of Mary, she was buried in a grave for the poor. Pope Pius XII canonized Maria Goretti and raised the little girl, who defended her purity, to the glory of the altars. Her mother Assunta was present for the celebration in St. Peter's Square. As Maria had done, Assunta forgave Alessandro, who had been released from prison many years later and sought her forgiveness. He repented of his terrible deed and died as a lay brother in a monastery.

Prayer of Blessed Miguel Pro, S.J. to the Blessed Virgin of Sorrows

Let me live my life at your side, my Mother, and be the companion of your bitter solitude and your profound pain. Let my soul feel your eyes' sad weeping and the abandonment of your heart.

On the road of my life I do not wish to savor the happiness of Bethlehem, adoring the Child Jesus in your virginal arms. I do not wish to enjoy the amiable presence of Jesus Christ in the humble little house of Nazareth. I do not care to accompany you on your glorious Assumption to the angels' choir.

For my life, I covet the jeers and mockery of Calvary; the slow agony of your Son, the contempt, the ignominy, the infamy of His Cross. I wish to stand at your side, most sorrowful Virgin, strengthening my spirit with your tears, consummating my sacrifice with your martyrdom, sustaining my heart with your solitude, loving my God and your God with the immolation of my being.

EIGHTH DAY

Mary—Mother of the Church

Invocation of the Holy Spirit

Breathe in me, O Holy Spirit,
that my thoughts may all be holy.
Act in me, O Holy Spirit,
that my work, too, may be holy.
Draw my heart, O Holy Spirit,
that I love but what is holy.
Strengthen me, O Holy Spirit,
to defend all that is holy.
Guard me, then, O Holy Spirit,
that I always may be holy.
Amen.

(St. Augustine)

Scripture Reading

The descent of the Holy Spirit on Our Lady and the Apostles

Acts 1:12-14; 2:1-4

Then they returned to Jerusalem from the mount called
Olivet, which is near Jerusalem, a Sabbath day's journey
away. And when they had entered, they went up to the upper

room, where they were staying, Peter and John and James and Andrew, Philip and Thomas, Bartholomew and Matthew, James the son of Alphaeus and Simon the Zealot and Judas the son of James. All these with one accord were devoting themselves to prayer, together with the women and Mary the mother of Jesus, and his brothers. When the day of Pentecost arrived, they were all together in one place. And suddenly there came from heaven a sound like a mighty rushing wind, and it filled the entire house where they were sitting. And divided tongues as of fire appeared to them and rested on each one of them. And they were all filled with the Holy Spirit and began to speak in other tongues as the Spirit gave them utterance.

Reflection

Christ's work on earth is fulfilled. With His blood He has paid a ransom for fallen mankind. In His resurrection, He has defeated death, and has opened the gates to heaven by His Ascension. He now wants to entrust to the Church the continuation of this salvific work on earth, since God "desires all people to be saved and to come to the knowledge of the truth" (1 Tim 2:4). Through her, the saving graces of Christ can reach all people in all times. Through the Magisterium of the Church, that teaches God's revelation, truth shall enter their hearts. Christ has promised to send a mighty aid to His Apostles: God, the Holy Spirit. Since the Ascension of Jesus, the Apostles have been united around Mary. They know that the Mother of Jesus is their Mother and their Queen. Together they ask for the coming of the Holy Spirit—the first Novena to take place in Church History, from Ascension Day to Pentecost. The Mother of God prays and pleads passionately for the coming of the Holy Spirit. She herself was already completely filled by Him, but she knew how urgently the Apostles needed His strength in order to continue the work of her Son on earth. Jesus entrusted His Church to weak men, and the salvation of so many depended on their preaching and their prayers. Mary, the companion of Christ through the history of salvation, understood with more clarity than the Apostles that her divine Son would live on in His Church, His Spouse. Through the members of this Mystical Body He wants to continue His work and bring it to completion. Through the Church, salvation will reach every person and all peoples.

The mystery of the Church is miraculously mirrored in Mary. As Christ is the only way to the Father, no one can find salvation outside of the Church, His Mystical Body. All the graces Christ grants to His Church flow through the hands of Mary. She is the Mother of the Savior and the Mother of the Church. Just as she cared lovingly for Jesus on earth, from heaven she does not cease to help and intercede for the Church. Both Mary and the Church, Gate of Salvation, Mediatrix of all graces are Mothers who tenderly love and care for their sons and daughters.

Like the twelve Apostles, she too pleads to her divine Spouse for the gift of the Holy Spirit to enable us to build up the kingdom of God. She wishes to mold us into holy apostles, who go out into the world to fearlessly preach the Good News and to bring His truth to all men, and love everybody with a heart inflamed by the Holy Spirit.

Let us be guided by Mary, Queen of the Apostles, so that in the power of the Holy Spirit we may serve Him as vital members of His Body. We cannot bring greater joy to Mary than to love the Church, the Mystical Body of her Divine Son, and to work and suffer so that the salvific graces can reach all people.

Decade of the Rosary

The third Glorious Mystery: the descent of the Holy Spirit on Our Lady and the Apostles

We pray to Mary for the powerful help of the Holy Spirit, for ourselves and for all shepherds of the Church.

Prayer to the Mother of God

My Queen and my Mother, I give myself entirely to you; and to show my devotion to you, I consecrate to you this day my eyes, my ears, my mouth, my heart, my whole being without reserve. Wherefore, good Mother, as I am your own, keep me, guard me, as your property and possession. Amen.

Closing Prayer

God, You have sent down the Holy Spirit upon the Apostles, who were gathered together in prayer with Mary, the Mother of Jesus. Through her intercession make us worthy to serve You joyfully and to proclaim Your glory in word and deed. We ask this through Jesus Christ, Your Son, our Lord and God, who lives in the unity of the Holy Spirit, one God forever and ever. Amen.

Spiritual Reading

The consecration to Mary serves the greater glory of Jesus Christ

The actual value of good deeds lies in the love, with which they are accomplished. Therefore St. Thérèse of the Child of Jesus says that one, even if only picking up a needle out of love, can convert a sinner. Mary has loved God more than all the saints. She has accomplished all her daily works and humble acts with unprecedented love and therefore has venerated God more with the smallest action than the greatest saints in their heroic deeds. What we give to her, she will pass on with this colossal love to her Son, and therefore venerate him more, than we ever could.

From the *Treatise on True Devotion*

If you live this devotion sincerely, you will give more glory to Jesus in a month than in many years of a more demanding devotion. Here are my reasons for saying this:

1) Since you do everything through the Blessed Virgin as required by this devotion, you naturally lay aside your own intentions no matter how good they appear to you. You abandon yourself to Our Lady's intentions even though you do not know what they are. Thus, you share in the high quality of her intentions, which are so pure that she gave more glory to God by the smallest of her actions, say, twirling her distaff, or making a stitch, than did St. Laurence suffering his cruel martyrdom on the grid-iron, and even more than all the saints together in all their most heroic deeds! Mary amassed such a multitude of merits and graces during her sojourn on earth that it would be easier to count the stars in heaven, the drops of water in the ocean or the sands of the seashore than count her merits and graces. She thus gave more glory to God than all the angels and saints have given or will ever give him. Mary, wonder of God, when souls abandon themselves to you, you cannot but work wonders in them!

2) In this devotion we set no store on our own thoughts and actions but are content to rely on Mary's dispositions when approaching and even speaking to Jesus. We then act with far greater humility than others who imperceptibly rely on their own dispositions and are self- satisfied about them; and

consequently we give greater glory to God, for perfect glory is given to him only by the lowly and humble of heart.

3) Our Blessed Lady, in her immense love for us, is eager to receive into her virginal hands the gift of our actions, imparting to them a marvelous beauty and splendor, and presenting them herself to Jesus most willingly. More glory is given to our Lord in this way than when we make our offering with our own guilty hands.

4) Lastly, you never think of Mary without Mary thinking of God for you. You never praise or honor Mary without Mary joining you in praising and honoring God. Mary is entirely relative to God. Indeed I would say that she was relative only to God, because she exists uniquely in reference to him.[15]

From the Lives of the Saints

St. Jean-Baptiste-Marie Vianney (Curé d'Ars)

This famous parish priest grew up on a small farm in Dardilly, France. As a boy, he slept in the barn. Up to the age of twenty, he served at home as an unpaid farmhand from morning to night. In the nearby city of Lyon, a guillotine was set up to execute priests, nobles, and other reviled persons according to the wishes of the Jacobins. It was during these years of the Revolution that John received his First Communion from a priest in hiding who celebrated Mass in his barn. When the revolution was over, John wanted to become a priest, but he was now too old. The simple mind of the poor farmer's son could not remember the Latin words that the pious priest from Écully had arduously tried to drum into his head. When he entered the seminary, he was sent home due to his poor aptitude. However, John trusted in Mary and her continuous

---

15. *True Devotion*, VI, 222–225.

intercession, of which he said, "She is even greater than the best mother!"

At that time, only one person—the parish priest of Écully—knew that there was something special about Vianney, and he could not be judged according to the norm. Together they fought for his vocation through of fasting, penance, and prayer. Against all resistance, they succeeded. On August 13, 1815, John Marie Vianney received his priestly ordination with the limitation that, due to his poor examination results, he could not hear confessions for a certain period of time. The young priest was also put under the supervision of his mentor. Among the priests of the Diocese of Lyon, he was a cause of uneasiness for the Vicar General and a target of mockery by his brothers in the priesthood. When the parish priest of Écully died, there was only one job that this "unfit" priest could take, serving as the parish priest of Ars. The priest there had just died of consumption.

No wayside Cross or Marian image awaited John Vianney in Ars. The Church was rundown, dirty, and there was not a single soul praying. Among the seventy houses in Ars, four pubs could be found. The new parish priest dropped before the tabernacle and rose to his feet the next morning with the firm resolution of winning the village back for the kingdom of God. He was convinced that silent and trusting prayer would work miracles.

In the beginning, the obstacles seemed insurmountable. On Sundays, only a couple of old women came to Church. Men sat playing cards in the pubs and laughed and cursed at the priest who would appear at their table reminding them of their Sunday obligation. Who did he think he was? The whole week they slaved away at work, and now this man dared to come and take away their Sunday enjoyment? The villagers resisted him even more and boasted that the priest would draw the short straw. But John not only fought for souls with words. Soon it was common knowledge that he had given away all of his belongings to the poor, that he owned only a worn cassock and did not even have a coat. It became known that he only ate potatoes, sometimes rotten, which he cooked on Mondays for the whole week. The priest was poorer than the poorest servant.

All the while, John Vianney struggled with God for the souls of his village. At two o'clock in the morning, he would wake up and pray his breviary. At four o'clock he would go to the church where he would remain until midday. He always prayed a "Hail Mary" at the toll of the bell every hour and venerated the Immaculate Conception. The whole day was truly an unceasing prayer. His trust in Mary was indescribable. He consecrated his parish to her and enclosed all the names of his parishioners in the heart of a Marian statue. She was his greatest love, so much so that he could utter, "God could have made a better world than ours, but no creature with greater perfection than Mary." One day, he confided to Catherine Lassagne, one of his spiritual daughters, these words: "I loved Mary even before I knew her; she is my oldest love!"

Soon, Mary rewarded his total trust in her, and fulfilled the words of her faithful admirer: "Everywhere the Virgin is venerated, she will perform miracles!" The village changed; the first to follow were the women and children. The men resisted at first, but then supported their priest eagerly. What had convinced them was the way he lived his life, in accordance with his words. From then on, the church of Ars was never empty, and no one dared to desecrate Sundays by working in the fields or wasting time in the pubs.

The call of the saintly priest bore incredible fruits. People from afar drew near to see the parish, of which wonderful stories were told. Many found counsel, help, and comfort from John Vianney. Pilgrims came not only from France, but from all over Europe and even America as well. They all hoped to go to confession with this priest, who after a long period, finally received permission to hear them. Oftentimes, Fr. John Vianney sat in the confessional for more than sixteen hours each day. On more than one occasion, he was carried out unconscious. He often recommended the consecration to the Mother of God, in a trustful prayer to her, especially when guilt and failure burdened the soul: "The glorious Virgin stands between us and her Son. The more sinful we are, the more compassion she feels for us. The child who most brings his mother to tears is most precious to her heart. Does a mother not always hasten to help the weakest? Does a doctor in a hospital not give the most attention to those who are the most ill?"

The Curé of Ars fostered a special devotion to the mystery of the Eucharist—God in our midst—in all its marvelous aspects: the sacrifice of the Altar, the silent friend in the Tabernacle, the food of eternal life in Holy Communion: "The food of the soul is the Body and Blood of God! Oh, admirable Food! If we considered it, it would make us lose ourselves in that abyss of love for all of eternity! How happy are the pure souls who have the happiness of being united to Our Lord in Communion! They will shine like beautiful diamonds in Heaven, because God will be seen in them." St. John-Marie Vianney was afire with love for Jesus. He desired that this spark of love would set others' hearts ablaze: "To know You means to love You... If we knew how much the Lord loved us, we would die! If they saw how greatly they are loved, I do not believe there would be hearts incapable of loving... Love is so wonderful! Pure love flows from the heart of Jesus... The only joy that we have on earth consists in loving God and knowing that God loves us..."

The parish priest achieved incredible success in his pastoral work also through his suffering. The devil assaulted and haunted him openly. Heavy attacks and slander attempted to

destroy the reputation of this priest. Furthermore, he had to
live with great veneration. People cut pieces from his cassock
as souvenirs and stole his breviary for the same reason. To
his dismay, the Bishop elevated him as an honorary canon of
the Cathedral. He immediately sold the violet cape in order
to give money to the poor. In the same way, he was burdened
by being raised to a knight in the honorary legion of Napo-
leon III. "All of that frightens me," he complained. "When
death comes, and I present myself with these trivialities, what
will happen when God tells me, 'Be gone, you have already
received your reward!'" This poor parish priest was certainly
received by God and His Mother, and abundantly rewarded
for all of his struggles when, on August 4, 1859, he closed his
eyes to the world.

Common Short Prayer of the Curé of Ars

O Immaculate Virgin, you obtain from God all that you wish!

Mary—Queen of Heaven

Invocation of the Holy Spirit

Breathe in me, O Holy Spirit,
that my thoughts may all be holy.
Act in me, O Holy Spirit,
that my work, too, may be holy.
Draw my heart, O Holy Spirit,
that I love but what is holy.
Strengthen me, O Holy Spirit,
to defend all that is holy.
Guard me, then, O Holy Spirit,
that I always may be holy.
Amen.

(St. Augustine)

Scripture Reading

The Assumption and Coronation of Our Lady in Heaven

Revelation 11:19; 12:1-5; 9; 17

Then God's temple in heaven was opened, and the ark of his covenant was seen within his temple. And a great sign appeared in heaven: a woman clothed with the sun, with the moon under her feet, and on her head a crown of twelve stars. She was pregnant and was crying out in birth pains and the agony of giving birth. And another sign appeared in heaven: behold, a great red dragon, with seven heads and ten horns, and on his heads seven diadems. His tail swept down a third of the stars of heaven and cast them to the earth. And the dragon stood before the woman who was about to give birth, so that when she bore her child he might devour it. She gave birth to a male child, one who is to rule all the nations with a rod of iron, but her child was caught up to God and to his throne. And the great dragon was thrown down, that ancient serpent, who is called the devil and Satan, the deceiver of the whole world—he was thrown down to the earth, and his angels were thrown down with him. Then the dragon became furious with the woman and went off to make war on the rest of her offspring, on those who keep the commandments of God and hold to the testimony of Jesus.

Reflection

John the Apostle, in whose house Mary lived, might have been her last witness as she made her way to her heavenly home. In the visions of the Apocalypse, the last book of Holy Scripture, he saw her gloriously transfigured.

Mary Immaculate was free from sin and all of its effects. She did not have to suffer death, nor decay in a tomb. When Pius XII defined the Dogma of Mary's bodily assumption into heaven in 1950, he left the question open of whether or not she had died. We may believe then that she, who was kept from the stain of sin from the first moment of her existence, did not suffer the effects of sin, death, or the separation of body and soul at the end of her earthly life. Since Jesus had died, she— the first among the saved—did not have to die. Because she suffered with Him on Golgotha and became the "Queen of

Martyrs," her final passage from earth was nothing other than a joyful passing without fear or pain. She is the perfect human being who fully reflects the will of the Creator as He wanted all men: without sin and without death. Her body, which had been conceived immaculate and which was nourished by God, was assumed into heaven even before judgment day, the day on which all bodies of the deceased will rise again, transfigured and glorified. Mary's Divine Son already took her up into heaven, body and soul, and embraced her in His arms with joy. The woman dressed with the sun, the most radiant and most honored member of the Church, had already reached perfection: she is gloriously victorious over sin, death, and the devil; she is the "great sign" illuminating the path of the pilgrim Church!

What blessedness it is for Mary to be united with Christ for eternity! Forever she is close to Him. What praise there was of the angels, as the Mother of God entered heaven! It is they, the holy angels, who adore God's humility, He who was born of a woman (cf. Gal 4:4) to become man! What wonder of the Patriarchs and Prophets as Christ led His Mother to His heavenly throne in order to make her queen of all saints? More glorious than all angels, more beautiful than the sun, unchangeable in her splendor, Mary sits on a throne beside her Son.

But even in her glory, the triumphant Virgin never ceases to be the Mother of her earthly children and to care for them. As Queen in the kingdom of her Son she uses her power to stand by her children in all of their toils. From heaven she intervenes in the battle, which the dragon leads with her progeny and proves to be the woman who crushes the devil's head. She is victorious over sin and death. In the last book of the Bible, this triumph of Mary, which was foreshadowed in the first pages of Holy Scripture, is fulfilled. The woman clothed in the rays of the sun, standing on the symbol of the adversary, the ever-changing sign of the night—the moon. "This woman has under her feet the moon, a symbol of death and of mortality. Indeed, Mary is fully associated with the victory of Jesus Christ, her Son, over sin and death; she is free from any shadow of death and totally filled with life. Just as death no longer has power over the risen Jesus (cf. Rom 6:9), so too through grace and a rare privilege of Almighty God, Mary has left it behind her and gone beyond it. And this is manifest in the two great mysteries of her life: in the beginning, having been conceived without original sin, which is the mystery that we are celebrating today; and, at the end, being taken up body and soul into Heaven, into God's glory. However, her entire earthly life was also a victory over death, because it was spent entirely at God's service, in the unreserved sacrifice of herself to Him and to her neighbor. For this reason Mary herself is a hymn to life; she is the creature in whom Christ's words have already come true: 'I came that they may have life, and have it abundantly'" (Jn 10:10).[16]

Mary is the sign of our victory. She is the immortal Queen of Angels and Saints. Despite all hardship, despite all toil and weakness we can now rejoice in her and build on the victory of Mary, which she told us herself in 1917 in Fatima: "In the end, my Immaculate Heart will triumph!"

Decade of the Rosary

The fifth Glorious Mystery: The Coronation of Our Lady as Queen of Heaven
With all angels and saints we rejoice that Mary is our Queen.

Prayer to the Mother of God

Hail, holy Queen, Mother of Mercy,

---

16. Pope Benedict XVI, *Address at the Act of Veneration of the Immaculate Virgin in Piazza di Spagna*, December 8, 2011.

our life, our sweetness and our hope.
To You do we cry, poor banished children of Eve;
to You do we send up our sighs, mourning and weeping
in this valley of tears.
Turn then, most gracious advocate,
thine eyes of mercy toward us;
and after this our exile,
show unto us the blessed fruit of Your womb, Jesus.
O clement, O loving, O sweet Virgin Mary.

Closing Prayer

God, You have given us the Mother of Your Son to be
our Mother. We venerate her as our Queen and trust in her
intercession. Let us participate in the glory of Your children
in Your heavenly kingdom, to which You have already raised
Mary body and soul. We ask this through Christ Your Son,
our Lord and God, Who lives and reigns with You in the unity
of the Holy Spirit, forever and ever. Amen.

Spiritual Reading

In Mary saints are formed

Sanctity is not something extraordinary for the Christian,
but actually the ordinary. "You therefore must be perfect,
as your heavenly Father is perfect" (Mt 5:48)—that is what
Jesus wants from us. To be holy means, to become Christ-like.
Mary, overshadowed by the Holy Spirit has formed the God-
man in her womb and has become like him in her sinless life.
When we hand ourselves over to her, she forms us quicker,
easier and better in the image of her son as anyone else. She
educates us and forms us to be saints, as the multitude of the

figures of history proof: no one amongst them that did not elect Mary to be his mother and queen!

From the *Treatise on True Devotion*

She is a holy place, a holy of holies, in which saints are formed and molded. Please note that I say that saints are molded in Mary. There is a vast difference between carving a statue by blows of hammer and chisel and making a statue by using a mold. Sculptors and statue-makers work hard and need plenty of time to make statues by the first method. But the second method does not involve much work and takes very little time. St. Augustine, speaking to our Blessed Lady says, "You are worthy to be called the mold of God." Mary is a mold capable of forming people into the image of the God-man. Anyone who is cast into this divine mold is quickly shaped and molded into Jesus and Jesus into him. At little cost and in a short time he will become Christ-like since he is cast into the very same mold that fashioned a God-man. They do not rely on their own skill but on the perfection of the mold. They cast and lose themselves in Mary where they become true models of her Son.[17]

From the Lives of the Saints

The Blesseds Jacinta and Francisco of Fatima

It was undoubtedly an unusual occasion when Pope John Paul II beatified the visionary children of Fatima, Jacinta and Francesco, on May 13, 2000. It is indispensable for every beatification and canonization to acknowledge the heroic virtue of any given servant of God, which towers above every normal Christian. After a long and arduous process at the diocesan level and in Rome, it must be recognized that

17. *True Devotion*, VI, 219–220.

the newly beatified person practiced the heroic virtues of faith, hope, and most of all, love, and that they extraordinarily distinguished themselves in the four cardinal virtues of prudence, temperance, fortitude, and justice. Martyrdom has always been regarded in the Church as proof of heroic virtue, but how could two young children, who died at the ages of ten and eleven, have reached this heroic measure of virtue? Certainly, kids can live as good Christians; certainly they can outdo other children in pious devotion and charity, but is it possible that they can reach a measure of virtue that puts them beside heroic figures and radiant examples such as the martyrs and the saints? The beatification of Jacinta and Francesco will refute the objection that small children cannot do extraordinary things with the grace of God and reach a heroic measure of virtuousness, which is granted to others only after many years. The blessed children of Fatima are an appeal to all Christians to climb the steep way of the imitation of Christ, that everyone is called to follow the steps of Our Lord with generosity—with Mary's hand, who wishes to guide all men to perfection.

The year the Mother of God chose to appear to three shepherd children in Fatima, 1917, is a more historic date than one would think. It points to the meaning of the messages of Fatima for the universal Church and the whole world to follow the call of the Gospel in all seriousness: "Repent, for the kingdom of heaven is at hand!" (Mt 3:2). Since the beginning of modernity man separated time and again from God, Christ, and His Church: in 1517, Luther nailed his 95 Theses to the church doors of Wittenberg and the Reformation which ensued split the unity of Christians in the West, separating the Protestants from full salvific communion with the one true Church. In 1717 Freemasonry was born, which asserted itself in the spirit of the Enlightenment against the claim of the absoluteness of Christ as universal Savior of all of mankind. The belief in the great architect of the world in connection with philanthropy replaced the Christian Creed, prayer, and piety. Finally, came 1917—the year of the Russian October Revolution and the beginning of nationally professed atheism, which fought for the denial of a supernatural being, not just against Christ and His Church, but the existence of God in general. "Religion as the opium of the people" was to be fought against and replaced by pure materialism, which was to guarantee peace, justice, and freedom in the phase of the class struggle of workers against capitalists: an earthly paradise without God, without Christ, and without the Church.

In the fateful year of 1917, in which in eastern Europe one of the greatest battles against Christianity too place, in the westernmost part of the continent, Heaven opened up to reveal its own strategy for achieving peace.

On May 13, 1917, the Mother of God appeared for the first time to the siblings Jacinta and Francesco, along with their cousin Lucia, in the "Cova da Iria," which is near the Portuguese town of Fatima. While Lucia spoke alone with the miraculous vision, Francesco could only see her, while Jacinta could only hear her. Not with violence and class struggle, not with liberal politics and shortsighted philanthropic action did heaven offer its own program of peace. Mary sees deeper and knows the true needs of men, and the problems which stem from sin against God. Therefore, in Fatima Mary starts her counteroffensive to save the world with prayer, penitence and loving atonement. No mighty men of state are invited on this mission, but instead, dependent, uneducated children: "Are you willing to offer yourselves to God and bear all the suffering that He wills to send you, as an act of reparation for the conversion of sinners?" Immediately, Lucia responds on behalf of all three children: "Yes, indeed, we do." The visions of the Mother of God, which occurred regularly over the following six months, changed the lives of the children forever. Mary chose them to be friends and allies in a special way, and the children answered her call with generosity and followed the plea of the Virgin with prayer and penitence. Magnanimously, they began to pray the Rosary every day. They fasted and did not quench their thirst even while tending the sheep in the blazing heat. They remained steadfast even while facing the insults of their own family and the villagers, who thought the children to be hallucinating when they spoke about their visions. Even when they were thrown into prison, and when they were threatened and intimidated, they remained true to what they had seen: a beautiful Lady dressed in white who had asked them to come to the Cova da Iria every month. In October, she would manifest her identity to them and perform a miracle so that all might see.

Already during the second vision on June 13, Mary revealed their early death to the two blessed: "I will soon come to take Francisco and Jacinta with me." This "soon" did not frighten the children, rather, it encouraged them to an even greater love for Jesus and Mary, fed by desire to see the beautiful Lady and her Son in Heaven for ever.

On July 13, Our Lady showed the visionaries a sight that some would deem unfit for the eyes of children. Lucia, Francesco, and Jacinta saw hell, where damned souls are thrown between columns of smoke and fire without being able to escape their pain, gruesome images that testify to the ultimate consequence of the denial of God. The most dreadful word of hell cannot be censored, since it makes the good news of Christianity visible and intelligible on the deepest level: Christ came to save sinners. Mary appeared in Fatima to remind the world of the great truths of the Gospel, to call for conversion away from the road to perdition, and to offer refuge in her. "God wants to institute the veneration of my Immaculate Heart to save the world!"

On October 13, 1917, thousands of people gathered
around the Cova da Iria to witness the last apparition and to
see the miracle that Mary had promised. The beautiful Lady
appeared to the three children and told them that she was
the Queen of the Rosary. Then something happened that was
visible not only to those gathered close by, but even to the
many witnesses spread out over a distance of fifty kilometers,
which constituted to be a unique sign, the sign that Mary had
promised as proof of the authenticity of the vision: the sun
began to spin and dance, emitting colors all around it, and
then ceased for a short while. The third time it seemed that
the sun was moving from its place and that it would fall to
earth. Screaming and praying anxiously the people fell to the
ground. Death seemed inevitable. Suddenly, the sun stopped
its downward spiral and returned back to its place. A sigh of
relief was heard from the crowd. The Mother of God had
shown that it was indeed she who had called the children to
the Cova da Iria month after month, and with the fascinating
and frightening miracle of the sun she had emphasized that
she had a message for the world: "Pray the Rosary every day
and stop offending God, who has been offended for far too
much already." It is man's sin that darkens the sky and plung-
es the world into disaster; faithful and childlike prayer will
lead to the promise that Mary had given to us in Fatima: "My
Immaculate Heart will triumph!"

As early as December 1918, Blessed Francesco fell ill with
the Spanish flu and Mary's prophesy that she would soon take
him to heaven became true. Francesco had to suffer great
pains, which confined him to bed and caused him to quickly
fade. Nevertheless, he did not despair but saw, in accepting
his sickness, the possibility of following Christ in His passion,
to manifest His love and to comfort Him. That is indeed the
core idea of Christian penitence: not blind self-reproach, not
closed and oftentimes self-centered asceticism, not depressive

fatalism and passive surrender to an inevitable fate, but a joyful "yes" to God's will, accepting all the good and bad from His hand, and seeing in suffering a true union with Jesus, Who suffered so much for mankind. To suffer and to love with the Savior of the world means making His Cross lighter and giving the Lord that which others will not. Francesco understood the profound Christian truth that the members of the Church will stand up, pray, and atone for one another, if they remain united to their head, Jesus Christ. In the childlike wish to "comfort" His Savior, Francesco mysteriously fulfilled the words of the Apostle Paul: "Now I rejoice in my sufferings for your sake, and in my flesh I am filling up what is lacking in Christ's afflictions for the sake of his body, that is, the Church" (Col 1:24).

On April 3, 1919, the Blessed of Fatima received his First Communion, the "hidden Jesus," as Francesco had often called the Eucharistic Lord in the tabernacle. On the following day, a Friday, he exclaimed: "See what a beautiful light there is at the door!" Mary had come, to take her child into heaven.

Soon afterwards, Jacinta fell ill with the flu. With amazing clarity and great fearlessness she realized that she too would soon die, and would have to suffer much. She told her cousin: "Lucia, Our Lady told me that I am going to go to another hospital in Lisbon and that I shall never see you or my parents again and that after suffering a great deal, I shall die alone. She said that I should not be afraid since she will come to take me with her to heaven." As was foretold, she was brought to Lisbon in January of 1920 due to purulent pleurisy, which required an operation. Her pain was seemingly unbearable, so that time and again the girl had to console herself by saying, "Patience! Everyone must suffer to reach to heaven!"

Jacinta had understood that the visions of Mary in Fatima were to be a reminder of the eternal truths through which man could be saved and truly be happy. That was the reason for which, on her deathbed, she said, "If men only knew what eternity is, how they would make all possible efforts to amend their lives!"

Jacinta suffered alone, separated from her family in Lisbon, but she knew that she was comforted by her heavenly Mother. On February 17, she saw for the last time the beautiful Lady, who had appeared to her in the Cova da Iria, announcing the end of her suffering. On Friday, February 20, 1917, Jacinta died.

We might think that the beatification of these two children, who were chosen to see the Mother of God, as something that can be taken for granted. We might deem it almost a logical consequence, as if the approval of a Marian apparition would be followed by the Church's veneration of the visionaries. Mary did not appear to the shepherd children of Fatima in order to prove their sanctity by miraculous events. Rather, Francesco and Jacinta were beatified because they followed the call of grace in a special way, by giving their definite "yes" to Mary's requests and by allowing themselves to be formed even if it meant suffering and trials. Not everyone has visions and not everybody can hope to receive a message from an angel, but God does not deny His graces to anyone; He calls everyone to follow Him.

Fatima is the urgent appeal of heaven for everyone to generously answer the call to holiness and to follow the steep path that leads to life, step by step, day by day, in the hands of Mary. The Blessed children have gone on the path before us. It was not too steep or burdensome for them, since the love of Jesus and Mary was alive within them. The message of Blessed Francesco and Jacinta is that love can change a seemingly difficult and trying life into a joyful imitation of Christ, making prayer and penitence like "child's play." The saints testify visibly time and time again, what Thomas à Kempis writes in the Imitation of Christ: "Love often knows no measure, but grows warm beyond all measure. Love feels no burden, takes no thought of labors; it strives for more than it can do; it makes no plea about impossibility, because it thinks all things are open and possible to it. It is strong, therefore, for everything, and completes and brings to accomplishment many things in which the one who does not love, fails and falls. My God, my love, You are all mine, and I am all Yours."

Act of Consecration to the Immaculate Heart of Mary

O Mother of God, and my wonderful Mother, tomorrow I will consecrate myself to your Immaculate Heart, dedicating to you my body and soul, all my prayers and deeds, my joys and sufferings, all that I am and all that I have, becoming all yours, Mary—*Totus tuus!* With a joyful heart I will surrender myself to your love. To you will I devote the services of my own free volition for the salvation of mankind, and for the help of the Holy Church whose glorious Mother you are.

O Immaculate Queen, my only desire is to do all things with you, through you, and for you. I know I can accomplish nothing by my own strength, whereas you can do everything that is the will of your Son, Our Lord Jesus Christ. You are always victorious. I implore you to accept my prayers and my humble act of consecration so that I might feel the effects of your triumph over the ancient serpent that you crushed under your immaculate feet.

O Most Holy Virgin Mary, inspire in my heart a fervent love for you so that nothing else but this true devotion will guide me in consecrating everything I have and all that I am to you alone. Grant me that tomorrow you will make my heart your throne upon which you reign over me. Let my soul be the shrine in which you will be venerated and loved with every breath I take. Accept me tomorrow as your instrument that you may use to advance the kingdom of your Son, who reigns with you, my Queen, for ever and ever. Amen.

DAY OF THE CONSECRATION TO MARY

Mary, my Mother, Queen and Advocate

The day of the consecration to Mary should be marked by a festive and happy atmosphere. If possible one should attend Holy Mass and receive Holy Communion, and follow with the consecration prayer. It seems adequate to copy the text of the prayer and to sign it after the consecration.

The consecration to Mary is tied to concrete intention for the future. These five should be among them:

1. To pray the Rosary daily (or at least a decade), as the Mother of God requested in Fatima.

2. To avoid sin with determination and to go to confession regularly, if possible once a month.

3. To renew the consecration to Mary every first Saturday of the Month.

4. To wear the miraculous medal or the scapular as outer sign of the dedication to Mary.

5. To foster the veneration of the Mother of God to lead as many people as possible through Mary to Christ.

Invocation of the Holy Spirit

Come, Holy Ghost, Creator blest,
and in our hearts take up Your rest;
come with Your grace and heav'nly aid,
To fill the hearts which You hast made

O Comforter, to You we cry,
You heav'nly gift of God most high,
You Fount of life, and Fire of love,
and sweet anointing from above.

O Finger of the hand divine,
the sevenfold gifts of grace are thine;
true promise of the Father You,
who dost the tongue with power endow.

Your light to every sense impart,
and shed Your love in every heart;
thine own unfailing might supply
to strengthen our infirmity.

Drive far away our ghostly foe,
and thine abiding peace bestow;
if You be our preventing Guide,
no evil can our steps betide.

Praise we the Father and the Son
and Holy Spirit with them One;
and may the Son on us bestow
the gifts that from the Spirit flow. Amen.

Scripture Reading

Luke 2: 22-25;27-28;30-35

By the hands of Mary to God's inner sanctum

And when the time came for their purification according to the Law of Moses, they brought Him up to Jerusalem to present Him to the Lord (as it is written in the Law of the Lord, "Every male who first opens the womb shall be called holy to the Lord") and to offer a sacrifice according to what is said in the Law of the Lord, "a pair of turtledoves, or two young pigeons." Now there was a man in Jerusalem, whose name was Simeon, and this man was righteous and devout, waiting for the consolation of Israel, and the Holy Spirit was upon him.

And he came in the Spirit into the temple, and when the parents brought in the child Jesus, to do for Him according to the custom of the Law, he took Him up in his arms and blessed God saying: My eyes have seen your salvation that you have prepared in the presence of all peoples, a light for revelation to the Gentiles, and for glory to your people Israel." And His father and His mother marveled at what was said about Him. And Simeon blessed them and said to Mary His mother, "Behold, this child is appointed for the fall and rising of many in Israel, and for a sign that is opposed (and a sword will pierce through your own soul also), so that thoughts from many hearts may be revealed"

Reflection

The time has come to bring Jesus to the Temple, to offer Him up to the Father. In the arms of His Mother Mary, Christ visits the Sanctuary of Jerusalem for the first time. Despite being true and eternal God and Lord of the temple, He allows

Himself to be carried into this holy space as an infant, in
order to fulfill the Law of Moses. Like the countless sacrificial
animals, which were a sign and a foreshadowing of the salvific
act of Christ, the Messiah, the innocent lamb who would be
slain for the salvation of man, approaches. "Christ, therefore,
entering the world says: 'Sacrifices and burnt offerings do not
please Me. Then I said, 'Yes, I come—it is written of Me in
Scripture– to do Your will, God'." (Heb 10:5–7)

Mary carries the sacrificial Lamb into the temple to offer it
up to the Father. The harsh words of the aged Simeon, that a
sword will pierce her heart, allow her to foresee that her Son
is unlike the Messiah that many Jews were awaiting—a shining
hero with military power that would cast the Romans out of
the land—but a suffering Servant of the Lord, Who carries
the sins of His people and gives His life to save mankind.

Mary brought the Child Jesus into the Temple of Jerusalem. She also wishes to guide us into the temple, into God's
sanctuary on earth, the place of His invisible presence, the
place where His everlasting sacrifice is being celebrated,
which was darkly prefigured by the religious ceremonies of
the Mosaic Law. Mary wants to lead us to the Church, to the
holy and saving community that her Son established on earth.
"The Church is our home! This is our home! In the Catholic
Church we find all that is good, all that gives grounds for
security and consolation!"[18] It is there—amidst the Church—
that she wants to take us in her arms and lift us up to God,
to bring us closer to Him and to consecrate our whole being
and life to Him.

Since we, as Christians, bear the name of the Messiah, our
great task consists in imitating Him ever more closely. That is
our vocation: to find Christ through Mary, to be at His side

18. Pope Benedict XVI, *Discourse at the recitation of the Holy Rosary and meeting
with priests, men religious, women religious, seminarians and deacons*, Aparecida,
May 12, 2007.

and to collaborate in the power of the Holy Spirit, to pray with Him and to suffer with Him so that His kingdom may come. He who consecrates himself to Mary, hands himself over to the Church, and places his life in the hands of God, showing his willingness to carry the cross in the imitation of Christ, and to not refuse it as so many have "who come to fall" (Lk 2:34).

Consecrating oneself to Mary means giving one's whole life to God in the sanctuary of the Church, to renew one's baptismal promises and to repeat the words of Christ that the *Letter to the Hebrews* places on His mouth, "Yes, I have come to do Your will, God!"

Decade of the Rosary

The fourth Joyful Mystery: The Presentation of Jesus in the Temple.
We ask Mary to accept our consecration, that through her we may become ever more like her Son

Hymn in preparation for the consecration

Ave Maris stella

Hail, Star of the sea!
Blessed Mother of God,
yet ever a virgin!
O happy gate of heaven!

You that didst receive the Ave
From Gabriel's lips, confirm us in peace,
And so let Eva be changed
Into an Ave of blessing for us.

Loose the sinner's chains,
Bring light to the blind,
Drive from us our evils,
And ask all good things for us.

Show thyself a mother,
And offer our prayers to him,
Who would be born of You,
When born for us.

O incomparable Virgin,
And meekest of the meek,
Obtain us the forgiveness of our sins,
And make us meek and chaste.

Obtain us purity of life,
And a safe pilgrimage;
That we may be united with You
In the blissful vision of Jesus.

Praise be to God the Father
And to the Lord Jesus,
And to the Holy Ghost:
To the Three one self-same praise.
Amen.

Prayer of Consecration

Hail, O immaculate Mary, living tabernacle of the Divinity, where the Eternal Wisdom willed to be hidden and to be adored by angels and by men! Hail, O Queen of Heaven and earth, to whose empire everything is subject which is under God. Hail, O sure refuge of sinners, whose mercy fails no one. Hear the desires which I have of the Divine Wisdom;

and for that end receive the vows and offerings which in my lowliness I present to You.

I,… , a poor sinner, renew and ratify today in Your hands the vows of my Baptism; I renounce forever Satan, his pomps and works; and I give myself entirely to Jesus Christ, the Incarnate Wisdom, to carry my cross after Him all the days of my life, and to be more faithful to Him than I have ever been before.

In the presence of all the heavenly court I choose You this day as my Mother and Mistress.

I deliver and consecrate to You, as Your slave, my body and soul, my goods, both interior and exterior, and even the value of all my good actions, past, present and future; leaving to You the entire and full right of disposing of me, and all that belongs to me, without exception, according to Your good pleasure, for the greater glory of God in time and in eternity.

Receive, O benign Virgin, this small offering of my slavery, in honor of, and in union with that subjection which the Eternal Wisdom deigned to have to Your maternity; in homage to the power which both of you have over this poor sinner, and in thanksgiving for the privileges with which the Holy Trinity has favored You. I declare that I wish henceforth, as Your true slave, to seek Your honor and to obey You in all things. Amen.

Prayer of Consecration to Mary

Nobody comes to the Father but through the Son,
Nobody can come to Christ but through you, O Mary.[19]
Nobody will be heard, if you do not intercede for him,

---

19. Leo XIII, *Octobri Mense*: "Like men cannot come to the Father but through the son, nobody can come to Christ but through his mother."

Nobody will receive grace and salvation, if not through you.[20]
Like the Eternal Word wanted to be all yours,
To redeem the world through you,
Equally I want to be all yours,
So that I can find through you, gate of heaven, eternal life.[21]

Therefore I choose you today, O Mary, as my mother and my queen.
It is you whom I want to give myself as your eternal good and possession.
Let my name be
Deeply written into your Immaculate Heart,
Which has never stopped beating for God and for us men.[22]

I want to give myself to you, all my body and all my soul,
my inner and outer possessions,
With all that I am and all that I have.
Yes, even the value of all my good deeds
Of the past, the present, and the future, shall be totally yours.
Totus Tuus!—I am all yours, Mary!

Accept me, although I am a sinner,
As your child,

---

20. Leo XIII, *Augustissimae Virginis Mariae*: "Her dignity is so great, God's love to her so immense, that whoever is in need and does not take recourse to her is similar to one that wants to fly without wings."

21. St. Louis-Marie Grignion de Montfort, *True Devotion to Mary*: "Through the blessed Virgin Mary Jesus Christ entered the world, through Mary he shall also reign in this world."

22. Bl. John Henry Newman: "Who can grasp that the virgin body, that never knew sin, should be submitted to the sinner? Why should Mary share in the fate of Adam, even though she never fell like Adam had?" St. Bonaventure, *Sent. III, d. 3 p. 1a. 1 q. 2*: "If the Virgin Mary was not tainted by original sin, then she also did not have to undergo death."

As your servant,
As your property,
So that you may protect and save me.
Without any exception you should have the right
To have me and all that I have at your disposal.

In your Immaculate hands,
let me be an instrument in this world,
That you may use as you wish
For the greater glory of God and the salvation of souls,
Because wherever you are loved and venerated
Christ's glory grows and his Church blossoms.[23]

O Mary,
In my weakness prove your power,
Which you have received from God as Refuge of Sinners
and as Mediatrix of all graces.[24]
Show yourself my Mother and the Gate of Salvation
Build through me the kingdom of your Son,
Who shall reign forever and ever. Amen.

---

23. St. Louis-Marie Grignion de Montfort, *The secret of Mary*: "We have to give ourselves over to Mary as instruments. Then she can stay in us, through us and with us, however she deigns right for the greater glory of her Son and through the Son for the greater glory of the Father."

24. Leo XIII, *Jucunda Semper*: "The most profound reason, why we want to win Mary's protection through prayer is without doubt because of her office as Mediatrix of divine grace. She acts in this office ever more, because she enjoys his highest esteem by her dignity and her merit. Her power surpasses all saints in the heavens by far."

    Benedict XVI's Address to the Marian Congregation of men in Regensburg on the 28th of May 2011: "To be Catholic means to be Marian."

Renewal of the Consecration to Mary on every First Saturday of the Month

In the consecration to Mary we have entrusted ourselves completely to the Mother of God, so as to find in her the quickest, most secure, and most perfect way to Christ, in order to form our lives according to His word. This demands that we follow Mary daily in imitating the Lord, that we always reach out for her hand time after time, and ask her to guide us.

The renewal of the consecration to Mary on every first Saturday of the Month, perhaps with a good confession, a time of silence, reciting the prayer of the Rosary, Eucharistic adoration, and the reading of scripture and meditation can be of help in order to not grow tired or indifferent in the spiritual life, but to go forward decidedly: with and through Mary to Jesus!

Prayer of St. Ephraem the Syrian (+373)

Hail, living temple of the Divinity!
Hail, immaculate robe of the One who is dressed in a mantle of light!
Hail, most pure one, full of grace!
Hail, you immaculate mother and virgin!
Hail, ornament of mankind!
Hail, fulfillment of the eternal plan of God!
Hail, crown of creation!
Hail, magnanimous throne of God!

Hail, source of the goods of life, source of Grace!
Hail Mary, Mother of God and Virgin.

Prayer of St. John Berchmans, SJ (+1621)

Holy Mary, Virgin Mother of God, I choose you this day to be my queen, my patroness, and my advocate, and I firmly resolve never to leave you, and never to say or do anything against you, nor ever permit others to do anything against your honor.

Receive me, then, I beg of you, as your servant forever. Help me in my every action and abandon me not at the hour of my death. Amen.

Prayer of Total Consecration of St. Maximilian Kolbe

Mary Immaculate, Queen of heaven and earth, refuge of sinners and our most loving Mother, God has willed to entrust the entire order of mercy to you. I, N…, a repentant sinner, cast myself at your feet humbly imploring you to take me with all that I am and have, wholly to yourself as your possession and property. Please make of me, of all my powers of soul and body, of my whole life, death and eternity, whatever most pleases you.

If it pleases you, use all that I am and have without reserve, wholly to accomplish what was said of you: "She will crush your head," and, "You alone have destroyed all heresies in the world." Let me be a fit instrument in your immaculate and merciful hands for introducing and increasing your glory to the maximum in all the many strayed and indifferent souls, and thus help extend as far as possible the blessed kingdom of the most Sacred Heart of Jesus. For wherever you enter you obtain the grace of conversion and growth in holiness, since it is through your hands that all graces come to us from the most Sacred Heart of Jesus.

V. Allow me to praise you, O sacred Virgin.

R. Give me strength against your enemies.

The Daily Rosary

In Lourdes and Fatima, the Mother of God asked repeatedly for the daily prayer of the Rosary. Even before those important apparitions, Saints suggested this ancient prayer. Blessed Mother Teresa of Calcutta, for example, explained that there is no problem that could not be solved with the Rosary in hand. St. Louis-Marie Grignion de Montfort also wrote in his small work, *The Holy Rosary*, on the importance of this prayer: before each decade, pause for a moment, however long or short, time permitting, think about the mystery that you will meditate on in the following decade, and ask for the intercession of Mary to give you the grace and virtue of this very mystery.

"Avoid the two gravest mistakes which some, who pray the Rosary, commit: The first mistake is that they do not unite their prayer to a special intention, and when they are asked why they pray the Rosary, they cannot give an answer. When praying the Rosary, always focus on some graces that you want to ask from God, some virtue that you want to acquire, or some sin that you want to uproot. The second mistake of the common prayer of the Rosary is when one wants to recite it as quickly as possible. This mistake emerges from seeing the Rosary as a burden, which lies heavy on one's shoulders when it is not prayed, especially when it causes a guilty conscience or when it is said as a penance against one's will."

It is distressing to see how most people pray their Rosary. They recite it with unimaginable haste and say their words carelessly. Not even the lowest of people would be met with such carelessness of words, and one should have the satisfaction of knowing that Jesus and Mary are praised by it! Furthermore, it is startling that the most sacred prayer of the Christian religion may remain fruitless and that one might remain the same after having recited it a thousand times— even tens of thousands of times.

Why does the Rosary take such a prominent place in the life of the Church? Why does the Mother of God propose it? The Rosary is the greatest school of prayer because of its simplicity. By the hand of Mary, the Christian learns, beat by beat, step by step, to speak with God, to hear Him, and to lovingly meditate upon Him. The Rosary unifies three types of prayer that, like steps, lead to an encounter with the Lord: vocal prayer, meditation, and contemplation. In other words, whoever prays the Rosary, prays with his mouth, his mind, and his heart.

Perhaps the prayer of the Rosary can be compared to playing the guitar. First, there is vocal prayer: the "Our Father," the "Hail Mary," and the "Glory Be." Saying these prayers is comparable with the right hand that strums the strings of the guitar with rhythm. But that is not yet truly music. Those who think that the Rosary is a purely vocal prayer—or worse still, a mindless repetition of many words—fail to comprehend it, just as one fails to understand that merely strumming the strings of a guitar is not yet a song. Along with rhythm, playing the guitar requires tonalities, which are controlled by the left hand. The same is true of the Rosary. Vocal prayer forms the frame of meditations on the mysteries. Like someone who uses his left hand to play chords in major and minor keys, the prayerful Christian discovers various tonalities within the Joyful Mysteries about the childhood of Jesus, within the Sorrowful Mysteries about His suffering and death, as well as in the Glorious Mysteries of His resurrection and glorification. There are always five chords in the rhythm of repetitious prayers, which bring the lives of Jesus and Mary before our eyes. During meditation we think about these mysteries and what they mean for our lives. In Nazareth, God becomes man through Mary; in Holy Communion, He comes to me! In Gethsemane, Jesus sweats blood. He suffers and is afraid as His friends fall asleep. Do I stay awake with Him, or do my eyes close…? On the morning of Easter, Jesus had risen from the tomb. The first day of creation had brought light. On the first day of the week, Jesus conquered death and gave us life. He can bring light within me, to what was dark before… Our prayer begins to become music, that is, it is not monotonous or boring, but instead rich in imagery, thoughts, ideas, and— if God so grants it—illuminations. The right and left hand playing the guitar, strumming the chords with rhythm, sound the different tunes of vocal prayer and meditation, of the lips and of the heart while praying the Rosary. One element is still missing for it to be truly good music, for it to be even deeper and a more profound prayer: the melody that the heart sings. Playing the guitar still requires a voice to sing the song.

Praying the Rosary also requires the singing of the heart that, in the rhythm and tunes of the prayer on the mysteries, presents one's own life to the Lord. Thinking about and meditating upon God becomes a resting in Him, in pleading or thanking, worship and contrition, childlike joy or apostolic decisiveness. The singing of the heart starts to resound when it prays the mysteries of the Rosary with a loving heart: Jesus, You Who were carried by Mary to Elizabeth, stay in my heart, let me be a Christ-bearer, because whenever I receive You in the Eucharist, I am a living tabernacle!… You were scourged for me. I have scourged You again and again. Please forgive me!… You ascended into heaven, Lord. I long for You, I long for Your kingdom, my true home…

In contemplation, the praying person sees the mystery before his eyes and lingers in special movements of the heart or affections before God. He sings his very personal love song in which he can and should include concrete intentions: You wished to be the child of a human mother, help my sick mother! You were crowned with thorns, help me in this financial distress that I cannot stop thinking about… You have sent Your Holy Spirit among us, without You I do not have the courage and strength to make good decisions...

The daily Rosary is—after the liturgical prayer of the Church, with the celebration of the Holy Mass as its center and climax—the most excellent means not only for one's personal sanctification, but for the conversion of the world. The string of beads is just like the slingshot of David—small and inconspicuous—but is an immense power, which can bring a giant to fall, that is the big problem and temptation of our time.

www.ingramcontent.com/pod-product-compliance
Lightning Source LLC
LaVergne TN
LVHW011234080426
835509LV00005B/491